ENCOUNTERS AND
DIVERSIONS

ENCOUNTERS
AND DIVERSIONS

BY

EDWARD V. LUCAS, 1868-1938.

> "I beg your pardon again when I
> disturbed you, but I hope not in
> wain."—*Letter to the Author from a
> Stranger in Budapest.*

Essay Index Reprint Series

BOOKS FOR LIBRARIES PRESS
FREEPORT, NEW YORK

First Published 1924
Reprinted 1972

Library of Congress Cataloging in Publication Data

Lucus, Edward Verrall, 1868-1938.
    Encounters and diversions.   Freeport, N.Y., Books for
Libraries Pr. [1972]
    v. 193 p. illus. 23 cm. (Essay index reprint series)

Reprint of the 1924 ed.

    I. Title.
PR6023.U24E6 1972   824'.4   70-156684
ISBN 0-8369-2560-2

PRINTED IN THE UNITED STATES OF AMERICA
BY
NEW WORLD BOOK MANUFACTURING CO., INC.
HALLANDALE, FLORIDA 33009

CONTENTS

ENCOUNTERS AND DIVERSIONS

The Sweep ᴏ   ᴏ   ᴏ   ᴏ

IT used to be a favourite device of humorous
artists—I think there are several examples
in Leech's work—to make drawings of chimney-
sweeps in close conjunction with persons of
superior cleanliness and fastidious attire. Indeed,
it is probably still done, for a belief in reincarnation
is tenaciously held among jokes.

But the odd thing is that, though I have seen
sweeps all my life—and a very early recollection
is of running out into the garden to watch the
brush emerge from a chimney—they have either
been on foot pushing their barrows, or driving little
carts, or about to begin their task in the sheeted
room itself. Not till last week did I ever see
a sweep sitting in a railway carriage next to a
person of superior cleanliness and more or less

fastidious attire. But I saw it then, and I remember the incident with some clearness, because the person beside him was myself.

He was a sweep of the old school. What the sweeps of the new school are like I have no notion ; but I suppose that they are as revolutionary as their contemporaries in other branches of art. Their rods, I should guess, are no longer straight but resemble corkscrews, their brushes are no longer round, and they probably maintain that soot is white. But my sweep belonged to the past, and in our conversation he lamented the changes that have come upon the world, not so much in the matter of sweeping as in the attitude of people towards those who perform that necessary task.

" I hope," he said, " that whenever you meet a sweep in the street, you throw a kiss to him."

" Certainly not," I replied.

He sighed. " Just as I expected," he said. " And there are very few left that do. But when I began it was still quite a common habit. I walked about having kisses thrown to me on all sides."

" But why ? " I asked.

" Because it's lucky," he said. " Didn't you

The Sweep

know that ? When you meet a sweep you should always throw him a kiss, and then you have good luck. Don't you want good luck ? "

" Want it ? " I exclaimed ; " want it ? "

" Well," he said, " that's a way to get it. But people don't seem to know it any more. I suppose it's because it's only the rules for bad luck that are talked about. Mothers tell their children all about spilling salt, and walking under ladders, and going to sea on Friday, and crossing on the stairs : all the things that bring bad luck ; but they don't tell them about the lucky ones. At least, only a few. They tell them about ladybirds or spiders settling on your hand, and about picking up pins, but they don't tell them about chimney-sweeps."

" Do you share in the good luck that you produce ? " I asked.

" Not us," he replied.

" But surely that's very unfair," I said. " Surely it's wrong that sweeps should be the means of spreading good fortune, but should have no one themselves to throw kisses to ? Isn't there anyone ? "

" Not that I've heard of," he said. " No, we just make good luck for others."

Encounters and Diversions

" But do you really make it for others ? "
I asked. " Have you any proof ? "

" Proof ! " he cried. " The stories I could
tell you ! Well, here's one. I remember one
morning, years and years ago, I was going along
Knightsbridge way a little after seven o'clock
—we begin betimes, you know—and at William
Street a lady on horseback was crossing the
road to get into the Row. She saw me and
blew me a kiss. A pretty lady she was too ;
a most beautiful lady. Well, I thought no
more about it, and I dare say as many as three
years passed when, one day as I was pushing
my barrow down Park Lane, I was stopped by
a lady walking beside a nurse who was wheeling
a perambulator, with the sweetest baby you
ever saw inside it.

" The lady looked at me very hard and then she
stopped me. ' I do believe you're my sweep,' she
said. ' Kate,' she said to the nurse, ' I do believe
this is my sweep. Do you remember,' she said to
me, ' my kissing my hand to you just by Albert
Gate one morning early about three years ago ? '

" I said I did. And it was true. There was
something about her that had stuck in my
mind all that while.

4

The Sweep

"'Well,' she said, 'I've been looking for you ever since. You brought me luck.' And she gave me a sovereign; for those were the days when there were sovereigns.

"'And might I ask,' I said, 'if the luck is in any way connected with this little angel here?' pointing to the baby. And she laughed and said 'Yes.'

"Well," he went on, "that's only one case. I could tell you plenty more. The gents who have backed winners after meeting me and have given me something for myself! Because there is some gratitude in the world, after all; or, at any rate, there was. I used to know more than one gent who said that he never had a bet except on the days when he had met a sweep."

"But suppose he lived opposite one," I said, "and couldn't help seeing him, would that count?"

"No," said the sweep thoughtfully. "I think it ought to be more accidental than that. Besides, gents don't live opposite sweeps. No, of course it must be accidental, because there's my missis—and no one could call her lucky. Rheumatoid arthritis isn't lucky, and she's

5

doubled up with it. And she sees me often enough. No, I think it has got to be accidental," he repeated.

He began to collect his implements.

" Well, good morning," he said at Victoria. " I get out here. I live in the Vauxhall Bridge Road."

And he left.

Glancing round furtively to see that I was unobserved, I threw him a kiss.

The Charity Song ～ ～ ～

"I HAVE just been to a Hospital dinner," he said, "and I'm so sure that the machinery for the extraction of money from guests is not yet complete that I have been devising a new implement."

"What is it?" I asked. "A pick-axe?"

"Not in so many words," he said, "but it corresponds. No, it's a song. An argument with music. I haven't had it set yet, but I've written the argument."

"I should have thought, from my own experience of speakers at charity dinners," I said, "that they left few arguments undeveloped. We should give because the object is the most worthy that could possibly be imagined. Whatever else might be questionable, this Fund demands support. We should give not only because we are generous, but even more so because we are just. We should give because

7

we are young, and the hospital is for the young. We should give because we are old, and the hospital is for the old. We should give because we are old and therefore shan't have many more chances to give. But you know it all."

" Yes," he said, " I know it all; but you don't. You have left out the real thing. You got near it when you said 'We should give because we are old,' but you missed the real point. You said that the old wouldn't have ' many more chances to give.' Now I am appealing to those in the audience who won't have *any* more chances to give."

" How do you mean ? " I asked.

" I'll read you the verses," he replied. " The time for the song is immediately after the last speech on behalf of the cause ; and you want a jolly unctuous kind of fellow with an appealing voice. He might make a living going from dinner to dinner singing it. It begins :—

In the state of London traffic.

But I ought first to say that the opening line can be adapted for the provinces too. In Birmingham, or Manchester, or any of the

8

The Charity Song

places that have three syllables, you would say—

> In to-day's congested traffic,

or

> In our city's awful traffic;

but in the ordinary two-syllabled places you would simply substitute another name for London. Thus :—

> In the state of Bradford traffic,

for example. In Bath you would say :—

> In poor Bath's congested traffic,

or ' old Bath,' if you preferred it. Forgive me for being so minute, but I am anxious that this song should be at home wherever people's pockets are being shot at.

" Now I'll begin again :—

> In the state of London traffic
> Who dare plan an hour ahead,
> Since it's so extremely likely
> He will be extremely dead ?
> In our whirling world of motors
> Who can call his life his own ?
> Every crossing claims its victim :
> Hark ! another dying groan !

But there is a silver lining, as we know, to every cloud :
To the wretch condemned to perish, mark the privilege
allowed—

Encounters and Diversions

Then the chorus, which says what the privilege is :—

> When a man's to die to-morrow
> He must reckless be to-day ;
> All may confidently borrow,
> None be empty turned away ;
> When a man's to die to-morrow
> How responsive he should be
> To the sacred call of Sorrow,
> To the cause of Charity !

" By this time," he said, " they've got the general idea, and of course it's a sound one. It was stated long ago, with more authority than mine : ' Eat, drink and be merry, for to-morrow you die.' I merely apply it : ' Eat, drink and be lavish as well as merry, for to-morrow you die.' How often I've heard men next to me at dinner at the Club say, ' If I were sure I was going to die to-morrow I'd have champagne this evening ; but, as I shall probably live for ever and I'm very hard up, I'll have a whisky-and-soda.' That is the notion. Very well, then, now for the second, or *ad hoc*, verse :—

> It is practically certain,
> Later, in the careless street,
> One of you, returning homewards,
> With an accident will meet ;

The Charity Song

You, perhaps, or you, or you, Sir;
　None can tell, but this we know:
This may be the last occasion
　Your benevolence can flow.
As it is the last occasion let it flow with all its might!
Pens and paper lie before you, and remember as you
　　　write :—
When a man's to die to-morrow
　He must reckless be to-day;
All may confidently borrow,
　None be empty turned away;
When a man's to die to-morrow
　How responsive he should be
To the sacred call of Sorrow,
　To the cause of Charity!

" ' Now then, Gentlemen,' the singer will
say, ' all together ' :—

When a man's to die to-morrow
　He must reckless be to-day;
All may confidently borrow,
　None be empty turned away;
When a man's to die to-morrow
　How responsive he should be
To the sacred call of Sorrow,
　To the cause of Charity!

" Loud applause, followed by the scratching
of pens. What do you think of it ? "

" I think it might be tried," I said. " I
think you should find a composer."

The Dead Hand

IT was that glorious time for Londoners—
the first day of the year on which the top
of the buses looks inviting—and, stimulated
and excited, I climbed up. After months of
inside—and why are they making the seats
just by the door so high? Half the male
passengers' feet, and all the female, dangle—
after months of inside it was wonderful to
have a dominant seat again, a place in the
sun once more, and watch the city unfold.
I began by playing an old bus game of mine
—betting myself some trifling sum that I
should see some one I knew before the end
of the journey: not necessarily some one I
knew to speak to, but by name; but this
was cut short by a talkative old fellow who
plumped down next me and opened fire at
once. On ordinary occasions I might have
monosyllabled him into silence; but on this

The Dead Hand

morning the vernal impulses were too strong : I was a universal benefactor.

So it seemed was he ; for his talk ran on nothing but altruisms. He had a newspaper in his hand and he pointed to a paragraph. It said that a certain lady who had recently died had left an old servant a legacy and ten pounds a year extra on condition that she looked after two favourite dogs as long as they lived.

It was headed :—

"LUCKY DOGS INHERIT."

" Every one," he said, " must have noticed how ready the papers are to print any odd thing in a will. They always even give it a headline : ' Curious Bequest,' or something like that, which they would never do if it were merely the gift of a living man and not of a dead. You know the sub-editor's instinct for adjectives—how he is never so pleased as when he can use such words as ' curious,' ' strange,' ' remarkable,' ' sensational,'—all certain as an attraction to readers. Very few readers can resist ' curious,' none ' sensational.' That's so, isn't it ? "

Encounters and Diversions

I agreed. I liked him. He was a new kind of bus-top talker. As a rule they only grumble at the traffic control or wonder who the dickens the people are who have time to spend half the day in theatre queues.

" Very well," he said ; " if publicity is always given to anything out of the way in wills, it follows that those of us who have to die and want to benefit posterity will have to put our wishes into testamentary form : ' Betterment by codicil.' Let that be our motto."

" But why won't the papers print such things about living philanthropists ? " I asked.

" They're afraid it might be advertising something or some one," he said. Very suspicious lot—editors.

" No," he resumed, " the hand that is to help must be dead. It is a wonderful opportunity for bachelors, old maids and persons with even only a little money and no dependents. What they do with their property now I have no notion ; but let them in future make their wills with an eye to social amelioration. It can't hurt them, and it may be of infinite service to the world they are disencumbering. Let them remember what the philosopher said to the miser : ' You can't take your gold with you, and if you did it would melt.' Remembering that, let them do a little good with it. Isn't that so ? "

Again I agreed. He seemed too good to be true.

" Now, looking round us," he went on, " what do we see that wants to be put right ? Why, here is a case immediately under our eyes—the hands of the bus-conductor. See how stained they are by the copper coins he is receiving and paying out all day. Isn't that horrible—a beautiful thing like the hand all grimed and discoloured, almost ruined ? Newspaper-sellers too—their hands are the same. Now how simple for some one to leave a few hundred pounds to provide gloves for those fellows ! And how instantly the sub-editors would jump on to it and spread the glad tidings :—

' STRANGE HUMANE BEQUEST OF
KENSINGTON RESIDENT.
GLOVES FOR 'BUS-CONDUCTORS.'

That might make thousands of persons emulous.

" And then," he went on, " there's an iniquity

that always enrages me—charging for programmes at the theatre. How ridiculous to pay half a guinea, plus tax, for a stall, and then have to pay sixpence more to find out who is in the play. And the poor people in the gallery too, who can't afford another sixpence—what a shame! A right-minded manager would either give programmes away or throw the programme on the screen before the start and during the intervals. Why, a restaurant might as well make a charge for the bill of fare! A legacy to the Actors' Benevolent Fund conditional upon such reform might sting the managers into decency."

" Would you go so far as to establish a fund to provide hot coffee to the ladies who sit outside the Gilbert and Sullivan pit doors from seven a.m. ? " I asked.

" No," he said, " I shouldn't. But I would like to do something to stop messenger-boys wasting hours there in keeping playgoers' places in the queue. That's not what that gallant little corps was founded for."

" You are a real social reformer," I said. " Anything else ? "

" Haven't you any suggestions ? " he asked.

The Dead Hand

" Looking at these lorries in front of us,"
I said, " I was wondering how long it would
be before every vehicle, and especially the
heavy lumbering ones that make such a row
that the driver can hear nothing, is forced to
carry a reflector. A sum of money left for
that purpose might make the authorities first
think and then act."

" You've got the idea," said my new friend.
" And what about fitting taxi-cabs with handles
to wind up the windows, and ash-trays ?
They've got to come, but very likely only a
dead hand will be able to effect it. Think
about it when next you look at your will. One
should always be looking at one's will with
an eye to helpful codicils like these. Good
morning ; I get off here "—we were at Chan-
cery Lane—" I'm going to see my lawyers
about something of the kind now."

" May I ask what it is ? " I said.

" I want to induce the Great Western Railway to put inside catches to their carriage
doors," he replied. " A large bribe, of course,
but worth trying."

17

The Food of Yesteryear ∽ ∽

IT is a fact sadly established in the sensory consciousness of all older people that the flavour of food, and in particular of meat, is not what it was before the war. Nothing is the same : I am aware of that ; but some changes, some deteriorations, are worse than others, and I place this one in a seriously prominent position.

Not only has the flavour evaporated ; the variety has gone too. We are in the hands of a ring ; a conspiracy has been organized to defeat the individual taste and compel it to join the mob. London has countless restaurants ; a few very dear and fashionable ; a few score that are dear and not quite fashionable ; and a vast number that thrive because they are cheap—the kind that every one is excited to " discover." The deplorable fact is that, save for price, all these restaurants are exactly alike in their menus ; they all serve precisely the same things. Beef,

The Food of Yesteryear

mutton, veal, chicken, rabbit (called chicken), and all the rest of it, day after day, evening after evening. Eating-out has become a habit; eaters-out are so excited to be eating-out that they can be bullied into accepting anything. And the result is this dreary monotonous round of obvious dishes, which, moreover, never taste as they should, either because they are badly cooked or because they are of inferior quality. Britons, who were never to be slaves, are slaves once more, principally to cynical Italian caterers.

Where are certain simple delicacies of yesteryear? Where is that ancient nocturnal amenity, the devilled bone? After the theatre, how agreeable it once was, too many years ago, to seek the Blue Posts in Cork Street and be sure of devilled bones! If the play had been good they came as a symmetrical savoury postscript to it; if bad, a solace. But where are bones devilled now; and, indeed, where are the bones fit to devil? Cold-storage, the friend of the modern restaurateur but the enemy of sapor generally, is peculiarly hard on them. Beef which, stiff and stark, has voyaged from distant lands and must be thawed before it is cooked,

Encounters and Diversions

is not the beef to bring bliss to the London play-goer. Few inventions have done anything to accentuate the simpler pleasures of life, and cold-storage least.

I am feeling particularly sore on this subject because the other day a friend from India, whom I was taking round London after fifteen years' absence, and whom I wished to make happy, expressed a longing for devilled bones; and they could not be found.

" Nobody asks for them now," said head-waiter after head-waiter.

" But if you announced the fact that you always had them, what then ? " I asked.

" I don't think so," he said. " People don't eat that kind of supper any more ; in fact, they don't eat supper at all except when they can dance—and then they don't want much."

Farewell then to devilled bones.

And to marrow bones, too, it seems, for I found it impossible on an impulse to give my poor friend that nutriment either. Only by ordering it some time in advance could it be obtained, and then not for certain.

" Nobody asks for marrow bones now," said the head-waiter.

The Food of Yesteryear

" But if you announced the fact that you had them, what then ? " I asked.

" I don't know that we could," he said. " You can't be sure of getting them good enough. They're things that must be good to be nice at all."

" You mean," I said, " that frozen meat . . ." but here, with perfect strategy, he found himself in demand elsewhere ; he had said too much.

And this, I suppose, is why every second-hand silversmith in London always has the same marrow-spoons in his window (there are some in Vigo Street that I have seen for years) ; no one needs them any more ; just as no one seems to want punch-ladles. Alas, for a decadent world !

But the self-protective ingenuity of the restaurateurs is not all ; there is a detestable snobbishness that is largely to blame. Certain dishes have become so unfashionable that if you want them—and they comprise some of the best food there is—you must either have them at home (after passages of not a little acerbity) or seek them in eating-houses where you will be too conspicuous if you do not wear your oldest clothes ; because—and this is the amusing truth—the best food now belongs to the poor.

I will make a list of some of the delicacies which false shame has excluded from the West End menus.

Pig's trotters.

Here is an exquisite flavour indeed, allied to a curiously attractive texture. But where can you get them. In Paris they are served regularly in the most gilt-edged establishments, and in Paris people are supposed to know something about food, although foreigners have done much to debase its quality. But in London pig's trotters are vulgar.

Sheep's trotters.

To some extent sheep's trotters merit the eulogy that I have pronounced on the *pieds de porc* : but they are less rich. As *pieds de mouton*, accompanied by a sauce called *poulette*, they occasionally are permitted to patter into a London restaurant ; but seldom. Most of them find their way down East, and remain there to spread delight.

Cow's heel.

You see how I run to extremities—but that is not my fault ; I did not invent the beasts of

The Food of Yesteryear

the field and their charms. Who has eaten cow's heel? (Dead silence.) But it is exceedingly good, and in the form of calves'-foot jelly is your favourite restorative when you are ill. Calves' head you have tasted on occasion, and have liked; but cow's heel—never.

And now we come to the word of dread; the word which you have been fearing; the word which leads to the most deplorable exhibitions of affectation or ignorance: Tripe.

Let us not inquire too closely into its source; but let those who are wise eat it and be thankful for a preparation at once so nourishing and delectable. As for the others, let them continue to shudder. A restaurant that always kept tripe, seethed in milk with its proper companions, and let the world know it, would prosper; and, incidentally, it would be an excellent place for Diogenes to carry his lantern to. There, at any rate, would he find sincerity, if not necessarily integrity, in the highest.

And that reminds me that if I possessed the three indispensable ingredients in any enterprise—time, money, and enthusiasm—I should try an experiment that I have often considered: I should open a restaurant where only one dish

23

was served. It has been done with great success, and it could be done again, because the world is always turning round. When I first came to London there were a number of small eating-houses known as Wilkinson's, where boiled beef was the staple. It was always ready, hot or cold, and you went there for nothing else. The quality was not that of the famous *Bœuf à la mode* in Paris—Wilkinson was for a humbler purse and palate—but it was excellent in its practical, cheap way.

The Wilkinson's were many, but there was but one Tyson's. Tyson's was upstairs at the St. Paul's end of Cheapside, an offshoot of a Manchester firm which, for all I know, still flourishes. The peculiarity of Tyson's was that nothing was served but chops and steaks, and nothing was served with them but hot buttered toast. If there is anything better than a chop or steak served with hot buttered toast—I mean such chops and steaks as were in those days— I should like to know about it. But Tyson's has gone, and gone are all the Wilkinson's ; the nearest things to them in specialization are Birch's in Cornhill, with its turtle soup and oyster patties, and The (or is it Ye ?) Old Cheshire

The Food of Yesteryear

Cheese in Fleet Street, with its two pudding days a week ; both some distance from London's restaurant zone.

None the less, I would, had I those three necessaries of the scheme, venture a restaurant to-day that should attempt a specialization similar to Tyson's. I cannot say what the one dish would be ; but my customers should be minutely informed about it by a sign-board before they entered, so that none could consider themselves ill-treated if no long *carte du jour* were set before them. Possibly the Irish Stew House ; possibly The Saddle of Mutton ; possibly The Pork Pie ; possibly The Home of Tripe. (And such tripe !)

Hoots ⌀ ⌀ ⌀ ⌀ ⌀

"OF course they won't get out of the way for that," said my friend, as his powerful car slackened down on our return journey by road from the delectable mountains of Dorset.

By "that" he meant the mild booming of the motor-horn, and by "they" a company of unruffled cows spreading right across the road and shambling from side to side of it: less than perturbed by our onset—deliberately disregarding it.

"If a motor-horn sounds exactly like the friendly cow herself—as this one does," he resumed, "why should she be expected to take alarm and give way? If you want to make a cow jump you must have a motor-horn that emits a sound that she dreads—such as a dog barking."

"Of course," I said. "Why haven't I ever thought of that for myself?" I added.

Hoots !

" What a chauffeur really wants," the road-hog continued—for he is a road-hog ; in fact, you have but to scratch any motorist, however gentle in exterior, to find that animal beneath his skin—" is something like an organ with stops. Without something like that he will never get the road clear, never have all the impediments removed. For warning other motorists and for the drivers of carts the present horn is more or less all right ; but it is the infernal creatures not on wheels that are the real trouble. Here are these cows, for example "—and it is true that the obstructionist creatures were still there, although by advancing at the slowest possible pace and now and then scraping a leg or a flank with our mudguards, we were gradually cleaving the obstacle—" here are these cows undismayed by anything but a dog's bark ; therefore there must be a stop in the organ to produce a bark. Next, what about sheep ? The bark would probably be all right for them, too," he added, " and for cats. But obviously it would never frighten a dog. For fowls and ducks you want a sound like a fox."

" And for foxes," I said, " a sound like a pack."

He looked sternly at me. " There's no need to be funny," he said. " Who has ever been

Encounters and Diversions

bothered by a fox ? Be practical. What other
animals are there that impede the progress of
the gods of the machines ? ''

" Pedestrians," I said.

" Well, there you come to a great problem,"
he replied. " Because pedestrians are divided
into so many varieties. For a large number
the best kind of motor-horn would be a gramophone which uttered the words, in as commanding a tone as could be mustered—the original
speaker could be a drill sergeant—' Stand still ! '
or ' Don't move ! ' Because it is the people who
start to cross the road and then, after pausing,
run on or back, who soonest reach the hospital
and the tomb. If they could be turned to
stone, so to speak, by the drill sergeant's decision
and timbre, the chauffeur could easily steer
clear of them. Do you see ? ''

" Perfectly," I said.

" Then there are the people who are too
shrewd and cautious to be run over but who
disliking motoring much and motorists more,
do their best, by crossing very slowly, to impede
them and force them to do the most depressing
and ignominious thing that can happen to a
driver—reduce speed. This class obviously must

28

Hoots !

be frightened ; but how ? You must find a sound that terrifies them."

" Why not carry a revolver ? " I suggested. " That surely would be simplest in the end."

" I quite agree," he said. " But the laws of this country are in such a mess there would almost certainly be trouble. Pursuit, inquiries, inquests : unpleasant consequences, anyway. Motoring will never be the joy it was ordained to be until a lot of vexatious restrictions are removed from the Statute Book."

It was at this point that the last cow was passed and we leapt ahead.

" But we are getting into deep water," he went on. " The motorist, I fear, will always have enemies until roads are made exclusively for him and pedestrians have tunnels to grope through. May that day soon arrive ! Me anwhile let cars be fitted with all the necessary s tops and horns ! "

At this moment our high speed suddenly vanished and our motor-horn began to fill the air with those distressing sounds which have done so much to endear this new form of traffic to rural dwellers. The cause of the delay was a leisurely motor-cyclist ahead, with a side-car attached, who was holding the crest of the road

—his only chance of a level passage—without giving the least sign of being aware that anything could be behind him wanting to pass. The side-car amateur has reduced this wilful unconsciousness to a fine art, and this exponent was masterly. He disdained pretence altogether ; he put up no affectation of being absorbed in conversation with his companion. He merely went on his undeviating way with the conviction that his own trifling conveyance was the only car on that road, or on any road, or in the world.

Well, we boomed at him for two miles, until, with the faintest suggestion of a smile on the back of his head, about his huge ears, and on each of his rounded shoulders, he turned down a by-road.

My friend was black with rage.

" That's where the organ and its stops are always going to fail you," I said. " It is not pedestrians who are the motorist's worst foes ; it is motorists. The triumph of the foot passenger is only momentary, but the driver of a side-car who wants to keep in the middle, right on the camber, can last out, at any rate, long enough to spoil your temper sufficiently to make your next meal disagree with you. And I expect he always will."

Secrets ◇ ◇ ◇ ◇ ◇

IN Bruges, not so long ago, I was examining, with the assistance of the old furniture dealer, a writing-desk of some antiquity. Fine as was the workmanship, rich and rare as was the old hard mahogany (*acajou*) from which it was made, and distinguished as was its shape, the excitement of the dealer was reserved for a minor detail. A secret drawer. In point of fact, two secret drawers. It was these that rejoiced him, these that set him skipping about and uttering sounds of ecstasy. And I don't mind admitting that they delighted me too, and should I become a customer it would be the secret drawers' privilege to turn the scale. For they were exceedingly ingeniously contrived, not only in their position in the woodwork, but because two other drawers, less secret but sufficiently secret to cause an intruder to pursue his researches no further, covered their lair.

31

Encounters and Diversions

Coming away I thought again of the fasci-
nation that the word secret always exerts.
" I'll tell you a secret." " Do you want to
hear a secret ? " " I promised I wouldn't
tell a soul, but I must tell you "—how sweet
these phrases are, even though the actual com-
munication means little or nothing, even though
we knew them before ! For too many secrets
carry no surprise with them. " Do you want
to hear a secret ? " says a pretty girl, all
smiles and eagerness. But what's the use
when she is so ostentatiously keeping her left
hand hidden behind her ?

If I were in the mood to be pedantically
logical, it could be shown that secrets that
are told are not secrets at all. Some other
word ought to be found for them. But ter-
minological inexactitude has a thin time in
a world with so active a newspaper Press as
ours ; and the Tenth Muse has never been
able to control her passion for " secret " as
a lure. Look, for example, at some of her
favourite headings : " Secret History," " Secret
History of the Week," " Secret History of
the War," and so forth. What she means is
Inner History, Hitherto Concealed History,

32

Secrets

or even Released History. Again, how we
jostle each other when she offers us "Secret
Revelations"; and could there be a more
mutually destructive pair of words?

But "secret" will never lose its power, and
for ever, when we hear of a new centenarian,
and rush off to interview him—I speak as a
Fleet Street adventurer myself—and he says
one of the two things that men who have lasted
for a hundred years always say—either that
they have drunk whisky and smoked all their
lives, or that neither tobacco nor spirits ever
made the faintest appeal to them—we shall
continue to entitle the article "Secret of
Longevity." But there was no secret—the
old boy had been boasting about it ever since
he was eighty.

It is a pity that the word "secret" has
come so often to suggest infamy, vice, or at
any rate something underhand and discreditable,
whereas it might just as well denote the other
thing. Thus, when the headline "Secret Life
of Dead Millionaire" greets the delighted eye,
the reason for the gleam is the hope—nay,
the confident expectation—of voluptuous, sor-
did, or sinister details. But why should not

33

Encounters and Diversions

the dead millionaire have masqueraded as an
angel of mercy ? Why should he not, as well
as his mansion in Park Lane and his manor
in Surrey, his yacht and his stud, have, under
another name, maintained a Home of Rest
for disabled clerks ? That would be a " secret
life " too ; but unhappily no caption writer
would draw attention to it in that way : at
most, " Dead Millionaire's Anonymous Bene-
factions." The precious word " secret " is too
valuable to be wasted on virtue.

As a friend to newspaper proprietors, it
has but two rivals, one of which is " Sensational " and the other " Mystery." " Mystery,"
indeed, is so nearly allied to " Secret " that
the sub-editor must often have difficulty in
deciding upon which to display ; but there
is a difference. A secret is a fact ; a mystery
is we know not what, and often merely an
invention. Secrecy, however, is of course an
element of it. I have no space in which to
pursue this alluring side-track ; but I might
say that the two best newspaper secret-mys-
teries or mystery-secrets of my time bear out
the contention that secrets should never be
told ; for both faded into nothingness directly

34

Secrets

they were investigated. One was the Druce coffin and the other was the Humbert safe. So long as those receptacles remained closed the thrill was magnificent : we thought of little else than the alleged load of bricks representing the body of the eccentric Duke of Portland—half hermit and half Baker Street emporium-keeper—and the alleged untold gold in the Paris *coffre-fort*. I wish we still had those unsolved romances of real life before us, to make our days more amusing. But how insipid when the truth was known— the poor innocent Mr. Druce's remains exactly where they ought to have been, and the Humbert safe as empty as the Hubbard cupboard !

And now there is Joanna Southcote's box. Personally, I think the trustees of the British Museum, or whoever is responsible, are foolish in not opening it ; but I feel very sure that all interest in that article will evaporate if they do so, and one of the very few secrets that can be called secrets will vanish.

The only true secrets are those which no one else can discover : that is to say, our own, the secrets which our own bosoms keep under lock and key, known only to ourselves, to our

Encounters and Diversions

God and, if necessary, to our lawyer. (Possibly to our lawyer's clerk, too, but that is one of those things that we never, for certain, know. Some depths must not be plumbed too far.)

But lawyers! I remember sitting at a public dinner opposite one of London's most famous legal advisers—the kind of man to whom you go only if you are guilty—and thinking what a terrible load of private information was concealed behind that gleaming shirt-front. Yet he seemed to bear it lightly enough, for he was as cheerful and conversible and convivial as anyone present. But what (I thought) a hullabaloo there would be should he suddenly lose control—he was then a great age—and begin to give his clients away! How such hostesses as were innocent would clamour for the pleasure of his company! What a rush there would be to sit near him!

It is often said that even the most scrupulous persons to whom a secret is entrusted make one exception, pass it on to one friend. This friend, I suppose, if he is sufficiently interested, makes his exception too, and so on; and yet the phrase, " I know it's safe with you or I wouldn't tell you," continues to be used and

Secrets

to excite pride and pleasure in the hearer. Analysed, the desire to tell one other person is not exactly a treachery, for often the reservation, although unspoken, is understood, nor does it proceed from any uncontrollable tendency to blab. The other person—the one exception—usually is so intimate, even so beloved, as to be considered almost a part of the teller's self, or at any rate as a sharer of the teller's life and therefore a sharer of the teller's secrets too. Such special leakage is a risk which all confiders of secrets run, have run, and will run. But most of them are aware of it.

It is one of the many facile sarcasms flung at women, that they are unable to keep a secret; but my experience is that they are, at any rate, not less to be depended upon than men. There are at least as many indiscreet remarks in clubland as at mothers' meetings.

To speak of myself, I am far more interested in the light than in the dark. I can be told secrets with perfect safety, and people round me who have secrets burning their breasts can feel assured that I shall make no effort to probe them. I am still unaware of the

Encounters and Diversions

identity both of the Man in the Iron Mask and the Gentleman with a Duster. I know that Sir Walter Scott was the author of the Waverley novels, but I am vague as to whether the writer of the " Letters to Junius " has yet been definitely traced. It was only the other day that I was more than startled by the disclosure that Mr. Arnold Bennett's first name is Enoch ; and yet I have been intimate with him all the century. This shows you !

To come back to the Bruges desk. Did I say whether I bought it or not ? But that is a—

The Invalid ✤ ✤ ✤ ✤

MY old friend Pernick was a few minutes late for lunch, and when he arrived he was pale and shaking.

Long before I could ask him what was wrong he told me.

"I've just come from Harley Street," he said. "I've been to a specialist. It's terrible. My heart's all wrong. I might go off any minute. I'm sorry if you find me a nuisance over my food, but I've got to be very particular," he said. "Only the most easily digestible things." He sighed. "It practically amounts to a death-sentence."

I shook his hand again in sympathy. "Well, we've all got to die," I said with the idea of being comforting.

"That's a very gloomy view," he replied, frowning. "And that reminds me—I must be most careful never to get ruffled, put out,

39

the doctor said. Any sudden rage might be fatal."

" All right," I said. " And now for food. We'll find something safe, and edible too, I hope ; and of course you'll have no cause for irritation. This is my lunch, anyway. Leave your hat and coat over there."

While handing his things to the attendant he talked a little with him, and I thought I caught the words " specialist " and " heart."

We went to our table and he seized the *carte du jour.*

Most waiters begin with the phrase " A nice Sole ? " but this one remarked, " There's *Lobster à l'Américaine,*" hovering with pencil poised.

" Now," said Pernick peevishly, " don't tempt me. *Lobster à l'Américaine* ! That's the most indigestible thing you can tackle. I've just come from a specialist in Harley Street, who says my heart's all wrong and I must be careful ; and you offer me *Lobster à l'Améri-caine* ! It's monstrous. And I adore it too ! "

I put my hand on his arm to soothe him.

" Yes," he went on to the waiter, " and you're making me angry. I'm losing my temper, and that may be fatal, he says. All the

same," he resumed, " I don't see why I shouldn't
have some of the claws. Lobster's claws are
about the most digestible things there are.
It's the back that's so bad for you. And you'll
see that nothing but claws are served ? "

" You shall pick them out yourself," said
the waiter.

" No, I'm not up to that," said Pernick.
" I'm ill. That specialist rattled me. You do
it. You're sure you like hot lobster ? " he
said to me.

" Go ahead," I replied.

" And what will you have to follow ? " the
waiter asked on returning from giving the
first order. "A nice chicken? A nice
enbrecote ? "

" Well, whatever you choose," I remarked
to Pernick gaily ; " it won't be this ! "—and
I pointed to the words " *Caneton de Rouen*."

Never was a facetious warning less successful.

" And why not ? " he asked with some
asperity. " Why not? Nothing's so good for
you as a slice of a duck's breast, if it's tender.

" Can you guarantee that it will be tender ? "
he asked the waiter, although surely in a restaurant this is a question that answers itself.

Encounters and Diversions

" Certainly, Sir," the waiter replied.

" Then may we have duck ? " he asked me. " Forgive me if I seem to be rather running this show, but on a day like this . . . I'm not quite normal, I know." He reached for the *carte du jour* with a look of infinite self-pity.

" Very well, then," he said to the waiter ; " duck, tender, sage and onions, apple-sauce and sprouts, and "—he looked down the *carte*— " no sweet, but for a savoury, mushrooms and cream."

" My dear Pernick," I began in remonstrating tones.

He held up his hand. " Don't cross me," he said. " Remember, I mustn't be crossed. And what about a dry Sauterne with the lobster and a white Burgundy afterwards ? "

" You order them," I said, and he did.

While we were waiting to begin, he saw Richardson enter, and he sent for him.

" I've very grave news for you," he said. " You'll be bowled out by it. I've just come from a specialist in Harley Street who says my heart's all wrong."

" That's bad," said Richardson.

" Yes, but that's not the worst," said Per-

The Invalid

nick. " I've got to give up eating anything but slops—it practically comes to that. Isn't that awful ? "

" Dreadful," said Richardson. " But if you're wise you'll do it. What I always say is, if you go to a specialist obey his order."

" Yes, yes," said Pernick, " I agree. I'm going to."

He enjoyed his lobster claws so much that he had a piece of the back too.

" No use being morbidly obedient to one's doctor," he said. " We're all different. A specialist seeing you for the first time can't know everything."

Unfortunately the Burgundy was not right.

" Corked, isn't it ? " he asked me.

" I don't notice it," I said.

He sipped and held his head on one side with his eyes on the ceiling. Then he sipped again and held his head on the other side with his eyes closed.

" Yes," he said, " corked."

He called the wine waiter.

" This wine is corked," he said.

The waiter prepared to pour some into another glass to test it.

Encounters and Diversions

Pernick stopped him. " It's no use arguing," he said. " If a customer says it's corked, it's corked. Get another bottle at once."

" But——" the waiter began.

" At once ! " said Pernick. " And don't make me angry. You haven't heard that I've just seen a specialist, and he says that on no account must I be made angry. Get another bottle at once. You should have backed me up," he added, turning to me.

" But——" I began.

" No," he said, " I was right. My palate never errs. But don't let's discuss it any more, or I may get heated. They're very slow with that duck."

At this moment another of Pernick's friends passed and was stopped.

" I've got very sad news for you," said Pernick. " You'll be deeply grieved. I've just come from Harley Street, from a specialist. My heart's all wrong. Seriously wrong. And I dare say yours is, if you only knew ; but the point is you don't know, and therefore you can go on having a good time. When ignorance is bliss. . . . But I know, and I've got to be careful. Self-denial is my line for the rest of my life."

44

The Invalid

" You're beginning, like every one else, to-morrow, I suppose," said the new-comer with a glance at the table.

" What do you mean ? " Pernick exclaimed. " To-morrow ! I'm beginning to-day. Don't be sarcastic with me ; I can't stand it. The specialist told me that to be made angry might be fatal."

" I'm sorry," said his friend, and passed on.

" Cynical beast ! " said Pernick. " I hate that kind of thing. And now for the duck ! But I mustn't eat more than a slice or two of the breast. See that I am sensible, won't you ? "

If I could not make him sensible, I could at least envy him his appetite. And then the creamed mushrooms ! But to my intense relief he did not sit on after he had finished them.

" I shall have my coffee at the Club," he said, " if you don't mind. There are a lot of men there who will want to hear about this. It'll upset them terribly, I'm afraid."

And off he went.

How little fun, I thought, can deaf-and-dumb men have when they too are sentenced to death by their doctors.

To be Let or Sold   ᧡   ᧡   ᧡

AN ingenious editor casting about for what is known to the priests who serve the Tenth Muse as " free copy " has been asking persons of eminence to tell his readers some of the things on which they have " changed their minds." I am not to be numbered among those to whom the invitation was sent, but had I been I might have replied that I no longer hold the opinion, expressed many years ago in a light-hearted essay, that looking over a house to let was a pleasure that never palled. To-day I feel differently about it : not only because I hope never to " move " again, but because I am older, because I have too many other interests, because other people either are not such a fascinating study as they used to be or I have seen enough of them and their ways. If I were ever now to turn aside and go over a house without the legitimate reason,

it would be to see what pictures were in it.
I should keep a very wide eye for the walls.
A great many pictures now in public galleries
were found in houses to be let or sold, and
there are several Vermeers yet to come to light.

The amateur house-hunter, as distinguished
from him who wants a house, sets out on his
quest far less to see the house than its occupants. I refer, of course, to houses in which
the tenants still reside : the empty ones are
negligible. Perhaps you did not know that
there is so much curiosity about : that there
are people with so little to do that they spend
their time in " looking over " houses out of
sheer idleness, inquisitiveness, or even mischief,
being no more in need of a new domicile than
a snail or a tortoise is, but finding a wicked
joy in visiting agents' offices—perhaps morbid
joy is the better phrase—and then presenting
" orders to view " : even, in a more than commonly depraved mood, asking the agent's young
man to accompany them. How should he
know, poor youth, whether their questions
about the distance to the nearest post-office,
the drainage, rates and taxes, and whether the
vicar is high or low, ring true or not ? How

should he detect that they have no more intention of throwing these two rooms into one, and putting another bath, " for the maids," on the top floor, than he has of depreciating any of the undesirable desirable properties on his books ? All, I have been told, that agents know for certain is that clients who appear to like the house they are looking at never return, but those who find fault with it may not impossibly do so.

I am not in a censorious mood, for how natural that it should be in other people, when all is said, that our principal interest resides ! We may pursue this hobby or that ; we may meet to discuss philosophy, psychology, religion, the new murder, or the musical glasses ; we may profess an eremitical aloofness; but the proper study of mankind will continue to be man, and our real curiosity will be reserved for other people : where they live, how the devil they do it, and on what terms with each other. That poem of Robert Browning's called " House," in which an earthquake brought down the frontage only, tells the whole story :—

" *You see it is proved what the neighbours guessed* . . ."

To prove their guesses right or wrong may be a dominant impulse of the frivolous inquisi-

To be Let or Sold

tive house-hunters; but the humorous would go, I. fancy, more to hear what the present occupants say, for the people in houses to be let or sold are, more often than any others, what are known as "priceless"; and they are never more so than when they are explaining their position. Human nature is rarely so amusing as when trying to get a house off its hands. Women at this task can be untruthful enough, but their untruth lacks the infusion of candour which a skilful male liar can introduce. A woman will say that everything is all right: the house is perfect; she will regret to her dying day having to leave it, but she must; and her reasons will be sound enough: she is going only because her dividends have dropped; she has to unite in housekeeping with a widowed sister at Leamington; she is settling at Nice by the doctor's orders. But a man will ingeniously admit a fault here and there. "I'll be perfectly frank with you," he will say. (Beware of that!) Then he laughs. "Of course I'm an idiot to tell you this," he continues: "a real man of business would keep it to himself; but there are a few days in the year—not many—perhaps six all told

49

Encounters and Diversions

—when the wind from that quarter touches you up almost unbearably. Beyond that I can think of nothing. It's really a wonderful place and we're heart-broken at having to go. But this cursed Government, you know. Taxation! You're lucky to be able to take it!" Then (beware of this too) he is almost certain to add: "I wish that you would promise me one thing. If you take it and if ever you want to give it up, let me have the first chance! If things are easier then, I'll come back like a shot. You'll promise, won't you?" This is very disarming, but the genuine house-hunter must be on his guard.

There are various means by which we can learn about other people, from the pages of *Who's Who* to dinner-table gossip, but none is more amusing than to go over their houses. That is why house-hunting is among the National Sports of Great Britain, even if Henry Alken never illustrated it. To the frivolous house-hunter, as distinguished from the genuine house-hunter, an Englishman's house is his museum and his secret *dossier* combined.

But all houses are not equally the key to characters. Where some tell you everything, some tell you little or nothing : perhaps because the owner's real life is spent elsewhere. In other words, you may be in the wrong house. Where some people never seem to belong to their houses, others are intimately linked with every room. I have a friend who has moved five times in the last twenty years, but all those five houses have seemed the same to me ; they have been so full of her personality that there was no room to notice anything else. All five houses have been so characteristic of her that one felt that the address " Olga's New Home, London," should be enough for St. Martin's-le-Grand, especially after its constant boasting about the sleuths that abound there.

At the other extreme are the householders who are merely lodgers, whose homes have no more individuality than a hotel ; and the hotel, of course, is the perpetual proof of the powerlessness of furniture to create atmosphere unless its own human beings are there too. For it is not enough to select an arm-chair : one must sit in it. You may take the cosiest room you know and replace everything in it, word for word, in an hotel sitting-room of the same shape and size, and instantly the spirit of comfort will evaporate. The reason, of course, is that people in hotels strike no roots. The French phrase for chronic hotel guests even says so : they are called dwellers *sur la branche*. The only way to make a house livable-in is to live in it.

I have never seen " Chequers " and am unlikely to see it unless as a visitor, but I always wonder what are the feelings of the Prime Ministers whose home it so precariously is. Do they really feel at home there ? Did Mr. Baldwin knock the ashes out of that incurably public pipe wherever he happened to be, or did he cross with solemnity to the fire-place ? For what one does with tobacco ash is the ultimate test. Speaking for myself, I could never be at home in a house if I had no sense of security as to my tenure of it. No one can have that in the last final sense, of course, because of the beating, increasingly loud as we grow older, of the Angel's wings ; but (short of death) without any stable feeling, how can one bring oneself to tell the builder to put a cowl on the smoking chimney, or the carpenter to mend the shutter ? These are the things we do for ourselves or not at all ; certainly not for the fellow who is going to turn us out at the next election.

To be Let or Sold

" Chequers," itself, will that too one day be to let or sold ? Will there always be Prime Ministers in that genre ? The surrender of Devonshire House a year or so ago was a great shock ; and Mayfair's inclination to follow suit can be learned by a walk to-day through any of its once so secure streets, where the agents' boards are as thick almost as the forest from which they were cut. The thought of the rich and the luxurious and the deeply-entrenched giving up their mansions leads to the other extreme. History, I fancy, does not relate what became of the simplest residence of all—the tub of Diogenes—when it was vacant after his death. It would be amusing to know. Was it cut up into souvenirs for young cynics —chips of the old homestead—or were efforts made to find a new tenant ? I seem to see the advertisement : " To be let or sold (by order of the executors of Diogenes, deceased) commodious, well-appointed, old-world tub. Would suit gentleman of retiring habits. May be viewed by appointment. Apply Messrs. Steady and Steady, Athens." Perhaps the Prime Ministers of the not too distant future will be lodged thus !

Within our Gates ～ ～ ～

" I HAVE been learning things lately," said little Mrs. Kingsbury. " Two things."

" Only two ? " I asked.

" Two is a large number for one day," she replied. " And, even though such knowledge is depressing, I'm rather bucked about it, because after a certain age one learns so little." She sighed. " But all in a flash last Thursday I learned two things. One thing I learnt was the best way to discover how different different people can be."

" Yes," I said. " And the other ? "

" We'll take them in order," she replied.

" Very well then," I said, " tell me how you learned the first."

" By letting my house for the summer," she said. " It's infallible."

" You don't mean to say you've let ' Meadow Peace ? ' " I exclaimed.

Within our Gates

"Yes," she replied. "Aubrey said he was very hard up; we had a lot of invitations; the children are off our hands—worse luck, for it makes it useless any more to keep up the pretence of being young; and so when a good offer came I agreed. It was a terrible wrench, but I gave way; but not, of course, until I had every kind of reference and testimonial. The people were said to be perfection : quiet, cultured and all the rest of it. No young, no dogs."

"I thought you liked dogs," I said.

"Not tenants' dogs," she replied. "You'd have thought," she went on, "that the same feeling for the façades of country houses would mean a certain similarity of character, wouldn't you ? I like the look of 'Meadow Peace,' and these people liked it sufficiently to pay a ridiculously high rent for it. Therefore, one would have said, they and I must be more or less the same somewhere. A fallacy ! Take it from me that the people to whom you let your house for the summer are less like you than anyone in the world."

"And how did you find that out ? " I asked.

"I'll tell you," she said. "A few days ago

there was reason to get some papers from Aubrey's desk. It had to do with a deed or investment or something masculine ; and as Aubrey refused to go, of course it fell to me. So I wrote to the tenants asking leave for the visit, and of course they said ' Yes,' and I went.

" It is a strange, horrid feeling," she continued, " ringing the bell of your own house, especially when the door is wide open, as this was ; but of course I did it. I was admitted by my own parlour-maid, who looked at me with an expression I had never seen on her face before—one half recognition and welcome, but the other half reserved for her temporary employers.

" The tenants had tactfully absented themselves ; and it's as well that they had, for I don't know what I might have said to them. For it was awful—terrible !

" You know those stags' heads in the hall ? the ones Aubrey brought back from Scotland year after year ? Well, they had all gone. Not a sign."

" ' Where are the master's trophies ? ' I asked Parker.

" ' They're in one of the attics,' she said. ' The new people belong to the Prevention of

Cruelty to Animals, and they couldn't bear to see them.'

" But that isn't the worst," little Mrs. Kingsbury went on. " In their place what do you think there was ? "

" Texts," said I.

Little Mrs. Kingsbury opened her large blue eyes in astonishment.

" Yes ! " she exclaimed. " But how did you know ? "

" I guessed it," I said. " It was a natural corollary."

" Yes," she repeated—" texts. ' The new people are very religious,' Parker told me. ' Would you like to see the drawing-room ? '

" I said I would, although I suppose I oughtn't to have done so. But I was never silly about what are called nice refined manners. Still, I'll never do it again. It's a lesson. You remember the drawing-room ? Rather comfortable and jolly ? Well, they have done everything to make it stiff, ugly, formal, repellent. That big chesterfield, for instance. Obviously the right place for it is near the fire, especially during an English summer, with the light behind the head for reading. How could two persons

Encounters and Diversions

differ about that ? But these can. These people had put the sofa against a distant wall. And they had brought with them what I believe are called hassocks.

" And then," she continued, " the other rooms. The billiard-table naturally was not used for its rightful purpose. ' They don't hold with billiards,' said Parker. The table was covered with big books, under which flowers were being pressed.

" But it isn't only that the furniture had been moved," she went on ; " there was a new atmosphere too. Their personality impregnated the place—governed it. Don't you think that rather remarkable ? Even if nothing had been displaced I should have known something was wrong. The household gods were all on their hind-legs : you felt it."

" Well," I said, " it's a tragic story. And what is the second thing that you learned ? "

" Surely you have guessed that ? " she replied. " That one should never visit one's own house while there are tenants in it. Fatal.

" And now," she concluded, " I'm wondering if the house can be got right again ; if the new spirit can be exorcised ; if the household gods will ever come down on all-fours again ? "

"Of course," I said. "The spaniels and Aubrey's cigars will soon see to that. But if they don't, you must give another house-warming. In fact," I added, with the inspiration that comes occasionally to chronic guests, "I think that all houses let for the summer, even to sympathetic tenants, should be re-warmed. Mrs. Kingsbury's re-warming party might inaugurate a most delightful new fashion."

The Bunch ꤟ ꤟ ꤟ ꤟ

IN a hillside vineyard above Epernay a bunch
of grapes was ripening in the sun of the
Marne, and as they ripened they talked.

Like many young things about to enter the
world, they talked of what might be their lot
and what they wished to do.

" You have a great destiny in front of you,"
said the Vine. " You are going to be champagne. You are going to be drunk only by the
rich—chiefly the new rich and the temporarily
rich. You will froth out of bottles at banquets
into beautiful glasses, amid flowers and silver
and rich dishes. Men in white shirts and women
with low necks will talk the more gaily for your
sparkle."

" Are we going to sparkle, Mother ? " asked
one of the Grapes. " How delicious ! "

" Yes, it's your special privilege. And you
will be very expensive. You will cost scores

The Bunch

of francs a bottle, whereas many of your relations in the vineyards over there will only cost two or three. You are of the elect ! "

" And what are the other places where they will drink us ? " one of the Grapes asked.

" All kinds," said the Vine. " You may find yourselves at weddings and christenings and at coming-of-age parties. The wine is not unknown at race-meetings. Indeed, it marks most festivities here and everywhere."

" I should like to be drunk at a wedding," said a sentimental Grape. " I should like to be in the glass which the bridegroom raises to the bride, who may be the most lovely of her sex and the most charming. But if that is not my good fortune," it added, " I should like to be drunk at the christening of their first child. That would be a life worth living."

" Very pretty," said the Vine. " But it is all a gamble. You might equally be drunk at a lunch party of financiers, where you will come in useful to dull some victim's judgment. ' When you see champagne at lunch suspect a swindle,' said a wise man."

" Then aren't we always the friend of man ? " the Grape inquired.

61

Encounters and Diversions

" By no means," said the Vine. " You can get into his head and make him do a thousand foolish things."

" But we couldn't harm women—beautiful women ? " the Grape asked anxiously.

" Yes, and women too," said the Vine.

" I should like to be drunk at the banquet that follows the settlement of the Reparations question, which the Vines are always talking about," said another. " There must be wonderful speeches on such an occasion. I should like to be sipped by the French Premier as he affirms his total satisfaction."

" You're very pessimistic," said a neighbouring Vine who had been listening, and who was famous for her cynicism.

" Why ? " asked the little Grape in surprise.

" Because," said the cynic, " none of you will get into bottles that are ready to be drunk for at least seven years ; at least I hope you won't ; but there may be exceptions." She laughed sardonically.

" Oh, how disappointing ! " said the patriotic Grape.

" It's a fact," said the cynic. " Isn't it, neighbour ? "

The Bunch

" Yes," said the mother of the little Grapes, " it is so. I hope that none of you will be consumed before then. You will be in bottles till then, or possibly not at all, for there may be something wrong with you. And even if you reach the bottle stage you won't necessarily be drunk in France. Many of you may stay here, but others will be treated with chemicals and sent to England, where they like us dry, or South America, where they like us sweet."

" But what would England do for champagne if she and France fell out ? " asked the patriotic Grape.

" Ah ! that's a question," said her mother. " She would have to drink what she's got and then go without."

" Are there no grapes in England ? " some one asked.

" Only the stupid fat ones that grow under glass," said a cynic. " None worth calling grapes. You can't have real grapes to make wine with if you have no sun ; and there's no sun in England. England has nothing but weather."

" Wouldn't England be very unhappy without champagne ? " the other asked.

63

" Very," said the cynic.

" And does France get anything from England in return to make her gay ? "

" No," said the cynic. " Nothing but tourists, and they only make her rich."

" And does she want to lose them ? "

" Not at all. But when people are angry they forget what is good for them, and what risks they run, and everything."

" Do tell us," the sentimental Grape asked the cynical Vine, " what the exception is. You said there might be a chance of being drunk before seven years."

The cynic laughed. " Not drunk," she corrected, " but made use of. You might get into one of those bottles of damaged wine which are reserved to be broken over the bows of newly-launched vessels, in which case you will fall straight into the dirty water of the dock."

The Bunch shuddered.

" And what about America ? " another Grape inquired. " Does she make wine ? "

" She used to make a little," said the Vine. " But she mayn't any longer."

" Mayn't ? "

" No, she's decided it's bad for her."

The Bunch

" Wine ? "

" Yes."

" But how can wine be good for one country and bad for another ? Are the French and Americans so different ? "

" I can't say," said the Vine. " It's beyond me. But there it is."

" And is America perfect now ? " the Grape inquired.

" Naturally," said the Vine. " Directly you forbid people to drink the juice of the grape they become perfect. It notoriously is the end of all trouble."

" Then none of us will ever reach America ? " the Grape asked.

" I think we have talked long enough," said the Vine. " I never had such inquisitive children before."

Fate Malevolent

"IT is idle to tell me," said the stern man, "that Fate is merely a tissue of undirected caprice. I am as persuaded that we can be the conscious sport of Chance as you are that Chance is blind. I had another proof of it only last week.

"Last week," he continued, "it was my bad fortune—or it may be good fortune—to lose the last tooth in my lower jaw. I express myself as in doubt as to the effect, beneficial or otherwise, because the people that I have since met have been divided into two camps; one camp a very small one, which applauds the good sense of myself and the wisdom of my dentist, and the other a very large one, which says that all this wholesale extraction is rubbish, a passing craze, and that I shall never cease to regret it.

"I have had a suspicion all my life that everybody's own dentist is the best and all others are mischievous impostors ; but never has that theory received so much support. 'What a pity you didn't consult my man!' is a phrase that I have heard twenty times a day. If I had any ivory left for the purpose you would find those words engraved upon it.

" All I can say at the moment is that whatever benefit may proceed from this dental operation, nothing but discomfort was the immediate result ; for with the last tooth went the plate also, and for a few days I was a pitiable object.

" Now, I don't want to probe into dark secrets, but I dare say that some of you know what a plate is, and are aware that, in order to pronounce certain words, especially those beginning with sibilants, two rows of teeth are important.

" Very well, then. I come to my point.

" You say that Chance is blind, that the Fates are innocent of deliberate mischief and malice. In that case will you explain why it is that it was not until I was without my full speaking apparatus that I found myself in a company that was discussing poetry and that foolishly referred to me as an authority ? And it isn't as if they were discussing poets that have honest patronymics, such as Browning and Blake and

Encounters and Diversions

Bridges and Byron and Marlowe and Marvell and Moore and Drummond and Patmore and Pope. I did all I could to keep the conversations to such as these ; but in vain.

" I ask you if it was not through some malignant and supernaturally diabolical pre-arrangement, rather than accident, that, within a few moments of sitting down, the lady next to me asked me to tell her the name of Mr. A. E. Housman's most famous book ? This work has been published for years and no one ever required me to mention its title before. They have always known it. Why should it happen on one of the first days of my life on which to say ' Shropshire ' was an impossibility ? Tell me that.

" I made some sort of an effort, but only to be further humiliated, for she then asked me what was my favourite place in Mr. Housman's county. Now, my favourite places are Shrewsbury and Church Stretton ; but do you think I tried to say so ? Not I. I said Ludlow, and in saying so told a lie and betrayed Salop.

" I again pass over some fairly thin ice, of which Shakespeare and Shelley were the constituents, and come to a final treachery on

68

my part, forced upon me by the same inquisitive female. ' That beautiful poem called *The Song of Honour*,' she said ; ' do tell me the name of its author.'

" Now nobody has much better reason than I to know that it is by Mr. Ralph Hodgson. But put yourself in my place—you who also have suffered from the new wholesale dentistry. To us, of all names, ' Hodgson ' is the worst, as in a second's time, mentally rehearsing it, I discovered. And here we have malevolent Fate again. The *Shropshire Lad* question might just possibly have been chance ; but the *Song of Honour* question coming so soon after settled everything. Clearly I was being pursued ; I was a victim ; the naughty gods were in want of something to make them laugh.

" You who have been plateless too, what would you have done ? There were two courses. One was to feign ignorance and say, ' I've forgotten ' ; the other was to take refuge among the friendly labials and pull the lady's leg. I took the second course. ' Wasn't it Binyon ? ' I replied.

" That was the end of that ordeal. But I was not through yet ; the gods not having

Encounters and Diversions

enjoyed sufficient mirth, worse was to come. Later in the evening my hostess, who is fond of abstruse matters, was speaking of a remarkable case of clairvoyance which she had read in the paper. She produced the cutting, but, finding that she had left her glasses somewhere, she asked me to be so good as to read it. You who know what it is to be without the lower row, will give me all your sympathy when I say that the first sentence began, 'A very curious instance of the working of what may be called the sixth sense '—and so on. But I did not get as far even as that. No sooner did my eye, foraging ahead, alight upon ' sixth sense ' than I extemporized the finest coughing fit of my life and passed the cutting to a neighbour.

" Blind chance indeed ! Intentional mischief every time ! "

The Eternal Problem ∽ ∽ ∽

AS I was walking the other day down a
Campden Hill road, very obviously on
my way to Kensington High Street, an odd thing
happened : I heard a whistle behind me, and
looking round was conscious that a fat man in
his shirt sleeves, whom I had just passed at an
area gate—unmistakably a butler—was beckon-
ing to me. I hesitated, thinking in my superior
way that there must be some error. But no,
it was at me that he was gesturing ; and so I
went back, when with many apologies he asked
me if I would tell a cabman at the nearest rank
to come to such and such a house. He would
go himself, he added, but he was rather lame.

Well, I said I would, and on the way I thought
much about the unusualness of the request :
why it was unusual ; why it should be unusual ;
by what right I had in the least resented it ;
what other men less amenable would have done.

Encounters and Diversions

I thought how very lame he must be to have been able to overcome the ordinary reluctance of servants to call for assistance in this manner— off their own plane, so to speak ; I thought of the gulf normally fixed between butlers in their shirt sleeves and people who wear the kind of coat that—with no wish or intention of marking class distinction—I chanced to be wearing. For when all is said, it is coats that determine social position, and, if they are good enough, make it very difficult for fat butlers in shirt sleeves to whistle to strangers who are wearing them and to use them as messengers. I must assume that my expression was so benign that it cancelled Old Burlington Street's sartorial efforts ; although that is not what is commonly said of it.

But most of all I found myself thinking of what is called the servant problem in general and the difficulty that so many persons (although by no means all) seem to be having, first in persuading young women and young men to come to their houses, and then to keep them there ; and I wondered how much of this difficulty was the fault of the employers.

Most articles on this problem adopt an attitude

The Eternal Problem

hostile to the servant, or, at any rate, if not hostile they suggest that anyone who prefers to lead a free evening and free Sunday life, even under irksome factory or shop conditions, rather than to subscribe to the restrictions of a household, with fixed evenings off and so forth, is unreasonable. That is the word : unreasonable. This is largely because the writers of the articles are usually those who are in the position of employers. My own view is that the wish of these young people to have more control of their own evenings and Sundays is natural, and I sympathize with it, but I also think they are wrong. I think that most of them would be much happier if they served for a while in families ; and although no doubt there are houses where discord and suspicion and impatience and even intolerance rule upstairs, I should guess that most families get to be quite good company.

As a matter of fact, domestic servants are better off than most of their employers, for they have few of their worries. Some of them have to cook the food and some have to carry it to table ; but all of them eat of it later, and none of them have to pay for it, as the master

of the house does. They have no anxiety about
their meals, none about their lodging, none about
income tax. Their wages are regular. They
always have a fire, whereas far too many mistresses indulge the distressing habit of allowing
the calendar to control the heating of their own
rooms : even the English calendar, and we
know what a one-eyed affair that can be ! Servants even have their laundry paid for. If
only they knew what the privileges of an ordered
and protected life were, they could be the
happiest creatures alive, instead of too often
specializing in grumbling and discontent, and
complaining of the distance to the nearest
cinema, and giving notice.

They ought to think themselves lucky indeed
to be lodged, nourished and paid, in perfect
security, in return for a few trifling services.
I know that often, when that mixture of weariness
and financial panic to which writers are sus-
ceptible attacks me, I wish I was in the soft job
of my friend James, who is called a butler but
is really the beneficent tyrant of one of the
nicest houses in England, situated among pine-
trees and herbaceous borders, with a cellar by
no means to be sneezed at and no questions asked.

The Eternal Problem

If anybody had any real liberty, any real independence, and owed subservience to no one, then the reluctance of people to be servants would be more understandable. But since we are all servants. . . .! Whenever I hear the suggestion that to be a servant is a humiliation I think of the highest personages in the land. If ever there were overworked servants, eternally engaged in performing offices of which they must be heartily tired, but doing them well and cheerfully, despite the exacting nature of some of them, it is the King, the Prince of Wales, and other members of the Royal Family.

I have never been a domestic servant, but I have done enough amateur cooking to have for professional cooks an admiration that can hardly be set down in words : first, for the fact that they can cook at all under the conditions of heat that an ordinary kitchen knows, and then, and even more, for their ability to preserve the rhythm of the meal : to send up not only the joint, but the accessories that go with it, at the same time, and to allow no long intervals in between. A cook who, on the day of a big dinner party, can keep her head, keep her temper, but keep no guest waiting, is a great

6   75

master, and if I were standing anywhere near
Lord Rothermere I should take off his hat to
her. In default of that, I take off my own.

Nor is my admiration confined to cooks. I
admire pretty parlour-maids, too, and know
how charming they can be, especially when
they are charming. In fact, any servant who
can smile is in an enviably strong position.

As for employers, it is impossible to lay down
any hard-and-fast rule. There are strange
anomalies in this matter, and where one employer can do nothing right, another, and
presumably a very selfish one, can do nothing
wrong. The art of dealing with servants is
one of the rarest, and I am not sure that it has
not to come as much by chance as that of painting
or music : one has it or has it not ; it cannot
be acquired. Without it you will never have
good service : with it you can get what you like
out of the staff, no matter how unjust your
demands seem, to others, to be. That bug-
bear of the basement, " overwork," is hardly
mentioned in houses where this art flourishes,
however incessant the work may be.

A wise woman to whom I was speaking on
this question said that in her opinion the mistake

The Eternal Problem

that too many mistresses make is not to allow
for individual peculiarity in servants. " Too
many mistresses who are untrained," she said,
" tell their trained servants how to do things ;
which obviously is absurd. A housemaid has
been prepared for her task, and has her notion
of how to carry it out, and probably would
carry it out very well in her own way. But she
is not allowed to ; a mistress who has never
been a housemaid in her life orders her about.
This annoys her, even exasperates her, and the
mischief is done." That seems to me to be
logical. " Again," the oracle went on, " there
is far too much adherence to cast-iron rules.
In how many houses has the rose room to be done
on Thursday and the blue room on Friday ?
But supposing the housemaid didn't want to
do the rose room on Thursday—she might not
be feeling well, she might have bad news from
home, she is as entitled to moods as anyone
else—what harm would be done ? The room
would be cleaned all right, even though the
time-table were a little dislocated. Elasticity is
imperative," she concluded.

My own experience is that the mistresses
who are best attended to by their servants, and

who keep them longest, are those who exact
most work and most alacrity from them, and
who maintain the sharpest division between
upstairs and downstairs. The best servants
much prefer to have this gap ; they are shocked
when what are called gentlefolk shake hands
with them.

But it is a delicate matter on which to general-
ize, for there are also the servants who are
miserable if no bouquets are flung to them.
Those persons who were sent to the perusal of
" Tancred " by the recent stage version of that
novel, or who had known it before, will remember
the scene early in the story where the famous
chef breaks down in his great task of preparing
the coming-of-age banquets because he has
received no word of gratitude or encourage-
ment from his ducal employer. He had strained
every nerve to make a marvellous dish, but not
a sign that it had given pleasure had reached
him. And then the tactful Lord Eskdaile
intervenes and completely transforms his gloom
into sunshine by reminding him that he is more
than a chef ; he is an ambassador of culture ;
that these barbarians are not ready yet, but that
as they taste and partake of his creations they

will acquire sweetness and light. The chef beams to hold so high a mission ! And, true enough, the next day the Duke sends for him and expresses his satisfaction, and all is joy.

All servants are not conscious artists, and all households do not contain a diplomatist like Lord Eskdaile ; but all servants have their jobs and make some kind of effort to perform them, and all households contain some one that corresponds to the Duke, and no harm would be done if praise were bestowed as often as possible (and even a little more) rather than as seldom.

The Complete Introducer   ᔕ   ᔕ

I AM persuaded of this, that the whole manner of introductions at luncheon and dinner parties must be revised.   A spirit of thoroughness must come in.

The other day, for example, I sat at lunch next to some one on whom I had no line whatever. Her name, which I misheard, as I nearly always do, conveyed nothing to me, and we talked odds and ends in a desultory way and were of no use to each other.   Afterwards I discovered that she was the wife of a public man for whose work for the blind I have a peculiar admiration, and on this subject I could probably have induced her to be very interesting.

I feel the risks of missing the best of one's partners to be so serious that I have drawn up a scheme for hosts and hostesses which ought to add enormously to the amenities of the table.

The Complete Introducer

I will suppose you to be a man and a guest. As you enter the house or the room—the house is better, because you will have more time to apprehend the matter—you will be handed a card which will run something like this:— First, your name. Then, "You will have on your right Mrs. Travis Remington. Her husband is alive and they are still neither separated nor divorced. He is a railway magnate. Mrs. Remington's special interests are gardening and water-colour painting. All her children are living.

" On your left will be Miss Rachel Twist, who once had a play about Savonarola produced by the Stage Society. She lives in Florence in the spring and summer, and is an authority on the Renaissance."

With this information compactly to hand, you would know where you were, and could tackle either lady with confidence and the certainty of making no particular *faux pas*, while it is possible that from both, since you know their strong suits, you might even acquire something.

Meanwhile each of these ladies has been handed a card, on which you and another man are described. Thus, Mrs. Travis Remington is

informed, " You will have seated on your right
Sir Alfred Carver, the famous surgeon. But
besides being a surgeon, specializing in the brain,
and the owner of one of the best collections of
Japanese lacquer, he is an enthusiastic humani-
tarian and he keeps a number of old and useless
horses at his place near Camberley, where they
spend their last days in comfort. Sir Alfred
is happily married but has no family."

Every one will appreciate the necessity of
mentioning these last details, so much conversation now turning upon the marital bond in its
various degrees of severity or freedom.

The notice to Mrs. Travis Remington then
describes you :—

" On your left will be Mr. Archie Punchible,
who is a bachelor much in demand in society.
He has never been known to eat at home any
meal but breakfast, and that only from Tuesday
to Friday. He has travelled much in the East."

Miss Rachel Twist's card naturally must begin
with you :—

" On your right will be Mr. Archie Punchible,"
etc., repeating what we have just seen, and then,
" On your left will be Mr. Adrian Scoper, who
is an amateur of music and one of the first

The Complete Introducer

authorities on Scriabine and other modern Russian composers. He knew Tschaikowsky personally. He also has some very remarkable aviaries of small birds and talking parrots. He is a widower."

Thus informed, Mrs. Travis Remington and Miss Rachel Twist should know how to play their neighbours, and some not wholly meaningless conversation should result.

I admit that the scheme will give hosts and hostesses a lot to do ; but then guests, if they are worth asking, are worth thought and trouble. The real difficulty will come when some one cries off and there is a last-minute substitute. But that might lead to amusing misunderstandings, and these are always to be desired.

A Revolutionary Proposal ∽ ∽

EVERY one must have been struck by the
prevalence of dishonesty. Yet we all,
by straining our memories, can recall isolated
cases of the other thing. The problem is—Is
it not possible to increase their number?

I have a suggestion towards solution.

It is at the moment impossible to open a
newspaper without being confronted by reports
of turpitude, from petty larceny to murder.
Wives (we read) have been poisoned by their
husbands, householders have been shot by
burglars, hotel guests and actresses have been
robbed, jewellers' shops have been rifled, con-
fiding women have been deceived by bigamists,
gold bricks have been sold to Colonial visitors,
signatures have been forged, Chinamen have
been caught selling cocaine, investors have
been defrauded, horses doped, and thousands
of small thefts have been committed. These

84

A Revolutionary Proposal

are daily occurrences, and all receive the reward of print. Is it possible—since so great are the uses of advertisement—that the knowledge that publicity is to follow may have had an inciting effect on all those malefactors, and that, were no reports to be published, this tendency to crime would diminish or disappear? That may be too fanciful a notion; but at any rate we can never know till we try.

Supposing a newspaper were published with no reports of crime in it whatever? Is that too anti-social, too restrictive, an idea! If crimeless journalism became the rule it might, of course, land certain newspaper proprietors in the Bankruptcy Court; but how honourable a way for a peer of the realm to get there!

But, if records of turpitude are considered still to be essential to our civilization, might not space—of course not equal space—also be given to records of acts of virtue? Then, if the incentive of publicity is a fact, virtue might increase and every one would be happy. This kind of thing (I have made the heading lurid, but in course of time the reader would be more amenable to such a title as " Sensational Placidity in Kennington ") :—

Encounters and Diversions

WIFE ARMED WITH CHOPPER.

Emily Tyler, 54, wife of a Kennington plumber, after many remonstrances with her husband for staying so late at his Club, lost patience and went herself to fetch him home, armed with a chopper. After extricating him from his companions she kissed him lovingly and led him quietly back arm-in-arm.

With these eyes I have more than once seen obviously needy persons standing at railway bookstalls, where, owing to the rush, customers' coppers have not yet been collected ; but they have picked none up. I have seen, in tea-shops, people sit down at tables just vacated, on which the twopenny or even sixpenny tip still remained, and make no attempt to pocket it. If those heroic creatures were publicly given credit for their valour in resisting temptation, would any harm be done ? Surely not.

All this is but exordium to the story of an incident which occurred to me the other day. I was in an omnibus going East along the Strand, sitting next the door. At a certain point somewhere near the Bush Building, while the conductor was on the top, a man seated at the far end rose to leave, and as he passed me he handed me a penny and asked me to give it to the conductor for him, and jumped off.

A Revolutionary Proposal

Here was a case of peculiar honesty, for there
are many persons of ordinary sound morality—
as between man and man—who, if the conductor
had chanced to forget to collect their fare and
they were in a hurry to get out, would look
upon it as a gift from Heaven and accept it in
that spirit.

Others might employ the arguments of sophis-
try. The rights of companies, they might say,
are notoriously less sacred than those of in-
dividuals ; it is an adventure, and an innocent
one, to bilk a bus ; the block at Wellington
Street, having been longer than usual, had
meant an even graver loss of time than Londoners have lately been subjected to, and if
anyone can induce the road-mending traffic-
congesting authorities to attend to their business
surely the omnibus companies can ! Therefore
not having done so they should be penalised. The
conductor had neglected his duty. And so on.

This man, however, was more scrupulous, and
he entrusted me with his penny. I am proud
to be able here to do honour to his action, and
if I knew his name I would print that too, and
his address.

But to such an extent are our minds saturated

Encounters and Diversions

with suspicion, so prone are we to expect dishonesty and indecorum instead of virtue, gall and darkness instead of sweetness and light, that I have to confess, with shame, that when I related this incident to a friend of mine—or one whom I had hitherto looked upon as a friend—she asked, " And did you give it to the conductor ? "

A world which, really, must be improved !

Unbirthday and Other Presents ✍

WHOEVER it was that said that all presents were nice, but " unbirthday " presents were nicest, was a philosopher enunciating a general feeling. The unexpected is never so welcome as when it takes the form of an unbirthday present. There are only three other varieties, the birthday present, the Christmas present, and the wedding present, and of these the wedding present is the least interesting to buy. Both Christmas and birthday presents, except where great devotion or admiration exists, can be mechanical too ; but the unbirthday present invariably calls for real solicitude and even excitement. It is possible to give wedding presents, birthday presents, and Christmas presents without any thought or affection at all : they can be ordered by post card ; but the unbirthday present demands the nicest care. It is therefore the best of all, and it is the only

89

kind to which the golden rule of present-giving imperatively applies—the golden rule which insists that you must never give to another anything that you would not rather keep for yourself, nothing that does not cost you a pang to part from. It would be better if this rule governed the choice also of those other three varieties of gifts, but they can be less exacting.

The unbirthday present, springing as it does from a desire to impart surprise and pleasure, naturally calls up one's finest feelings : one is going out of one's way to be a benefactor ; one is even enjoying it too, practically participating in it ; but the birthday present is a matter of routine, and its recipient can be so different from yourself that it might actually be a mistake to choose for her anything that you could bear to be seen dead with, as we say. For your dominating thought must be not to improve her taste but to gratify it. There are friends and relations—chiefly relations—whose taste is too deplorable to encourage, and to these you may safely give things that are above them ; but for the most part the proper plan is to give people what they would like best. When, how-

Unbirthday and other Presents

ever, the special occasion arises, give only what you yourself like best.

The unbirthday present is peculiar in having two distinct origins. It may materialize from the wish to mark a friendship, to underline a recent experience, to provide a laugh or a thrill. Ordinary presents are sought for because dates are drawing near on which certain persons expect to be made the recipients of our bounty. The procedure is to remember that So-and-so's birthday is approaching and to set forth to find something for it. But with the unbirthday present this procedure is, in many cases, reversed : it is the sight of something in a shop window which that dear little Mrs. Mumby (to whom you wouldn't be giving presents at all if you were wise) " would rejoice in," or which was " absolutely made for " Uncle Dick, that impels us to generosity. The steady search for something suitable for Aunt Matilda on her birthday, or Cousin Rachel on her marriage, or the twins for Christmas, can be amusing enough, but the sudden inspirations that fructify in unbirthday presents carry more fun or emotion and make benevolence more electric. I can think of no more delightful existence than to be a new Haroun

al-Raschid with a passion for distributing anonymous and blue-sky gifts of this kind among
those by whom they would be most valued.

There are certain things which should never
be given as presents at all ; which we should
either buy for ourselves or do without. Pictures,
for example. It is very precarious to give anyone
a picture. If you yourself admire it, probably
its new owner won't, because two persons seldom
agree in the appreciation of art ; and if you
admire it excessively, your duty is to keep it
—your duty both to yourself and to the artist.
Scent, again : unless you are sure that the scent
you choose will be welcome, never give it. The
same remark applies to cigars ; but it is late
in the day to say anything about the danger
of a wife choosing her husband's cigars for him.
Professional humorists have been doing their
worst with that melancholy topic for many a
weary year. Neckties too.

The present that requires thought and even
imagination will always be difficult to select ;
but the present that is just a present is a far
simpler matter to-day than it was, say, twenty
years ago. Twenty years ago, if you wanted
to give a man anything, you gave him a cigar-

ette case or holder, or a match-box. A woman
needed a greater exercise of brains. But to-day,
when every woman smokes, you give a woman
a cigarette-case, holder, or match-box also.
And Dean Inge has been saying there is no
progress !

Of the three mechanical kinds of present—
birthday, wedding, and Christmas—the wedding
present is the most perfunctory, but a few heroes
are left ; the bull-dog breed is not extinct.
" Are you going to the Blanks' wedding ? " I
asked a friend the other day. " No," he said ;
" but I was invited." " Then you've got to
give a present ? " I remarked. " No," he said ;
" I hate them both."

What one gives to bridegrooms, I have no
recollection ; but for brides I once invented a
wedding present which appears always to afford
satisfaction. I have to say " appears," because
how is the giver to know for certain, thanks for
presents being invariably expressed in the same
terms of cordiality if not of positive ecstasy ?
For no matter what we give our friends
when they take the plunge into the dubious
waters of matrimony, or on the anniversary of
their own or our Lord's nativity, we are always

assured that the article was ideally chosen and
that it filled an aching void. But the wedding
present which I invented and which always has
appeared to afford satisfaction consists of an
old box that has pretensions to beauty—no
matter of what it is made : ivory, brocade,
silver, coloured glass—in which I place three
pounds worth of postage stamps, each one
carefully torn off. The stamps, it is true, in
the course of time, disappear (perhaps I ought
to endow these gifts ?—that is a serious thought),
but the boxes remain. They have to be beautiful enough to justify a long life ; and in the
search for them one can have a good deal of
fun.

Incidentally one may also become bankrupt,
because in the progress of the hunt, which
naturally takes one sooner or later to Beauchamp
Place and other similar danger zones, one sees
so many other fascinating things. For those
whose will is weak, whose purse is slender, and
whose acquisitiveness or generosity is highly
developed, London is at the moment no safe
city. Such recently has been the multiplication
of curiosity shops and the improvement in the
taste of their proprietors (there is a most seduc-

tive new bunch of them in Lower Grosvenor
Place, for example), that it is wisest to bandage
one's eyes or stay indoors altogether. In any
case, to carry a pocket cheque-book in these
neighbourhoods is, unless one is a millionaire,
a peril indeed.

While on the subject of cheque-books I should
like to ask why it is that, so far as I know, only
one London shopkeeper—and his shop is perhaps the most famous resort of those who would
buy new presents—keeps a cheque-block on
every counter ? What the firm's losses may be
by this alluring device I have no idea : perhaps
the " drawer " never has to be " referred to "
at all ; but the extra sales that come about
through it must be enormous. It is a clever
shop in other ways, too, for as you set your
foot on the entrance mat the door mechanically
opens. How wise that is—to welcome the
coming victim ! Perhaps if all such shops
adopted these plans, the giving of presents
would be gloriously increased and the happiness
of the world doubled.

The Voice of the Hand   ᔑ   ᔑ

I WAS reading the other day a murder mystery
story in which most of the running was made
by a masterly elderly French detective, whose
private hobby was rose-growing. One of his
remarks abides with me. So tell-tale, he said,
are the eyes, that if the whole world wore a
yashmak he would still be able to make accurate
deductions as to guilt or innocence. This struck
me as being rather sweeping. Trained observers
like this marvellous Monsieur Boulot (if there
are any) may be willing to dispense with the
testimony, and even the corroboration, of mouths
and hands, but I personally should need them
as evidence, too. Hands tell so much. It
would be wrong to say that one looks at hands
before eyes, but very soon after. In railway
carriages they can be far more interesting than
the morning paper.

I wonder if the beauty of hands is less considered than once it was. I suspect it may be,

96

The Voice of the Hand

because one of my earliest recollections is of
being told that a pair of hands in porcelain on
a table in the drawing-room were an exact
model of those of the Countess of Dudley of that
day. Well, the world now pays much more
homage to lovely women than it did even then,
and yet I have never seen porcelain models of
the hands of any of our recent reigning beauties.

The last model that I recollect seeing was
the plaster cast of Thomas Carlyle's hand at
the little Carlyle museum in Chelsea, very delicate
and nervous. And yet, that hands in repro-
duction are still not without their appeal is
proved by the constant demand which, I am
informed, there is in art shops for photographs
of that drawing of hands joined in prayer from
one of Dürer's notebooks. But, of course, it
may be the religious signification of the picture
that gives it its vogue.

Conjurers' hands, and particularly the conjurers who are clever with coins and cards, can
be almost separate individualities ; you forget
the man as you watch, and think of his hands
as magicians on their own behalf. As a boy,
how I toiled to emulate the gifted elders who
were able to make shadow animals ! I admire

97

them from afar still, but not with the passion
with which I admire the pianist who plays from
ear, surely the most remarkable of God's creatures ! Had I never endured the misery—almost
the agony—of music lessons, I might admire
them less ; but knowing with what difficulty I
could hit the right note, even with the most
careful thought and after great hesitation—and
even then probably hitting the next one with
it—I am the more bewildered by this easy
ability, and ashamed at my lack of it.

To this day every pianist seems to me mira-
culous ; but the pianist from ear, the pianist
who can instantly reproduce the tunes from the
musical comedy you have just seen together for
the first time—he is a demi-god. For such a
power as that I would give anything that I
have. Which reminds me that the Creator must
smile a little when he thinks of the range of
activities which the hands that He made, chiefly,
as I suppose, to delve, to spin, and to convey
food to the mouth, have added to those primitive
functions. The hands, for example, of Tom
Newman and Ignace Paderewski, the hands of
Augustus John, the hands of that most accomp-
lished of living jugglers, Rastelli, the battered

The Voice of the Hand

hands of Harry Strudwick, the conquering hands of Jack Dempsey. But fisticuffs, of course, are no new development; they began almost when the world began. I have had, by the way, the honour of meeting Jack Dempsey on a social occasion, and I can assure you that when I laid my own not inconsiderable paw in his, it looked like a leaf in the storm.

There used to be a joke, in the days when jokes about the Chosen People were more common than now, that if you tied a Jew's hands to his sides you made him dumb. But it would be more true of the Latin people, whose manual gestures are far more varied and constant. An Englishman and an American can describe a fight, a motor accident or a Rugby match—in fact anything but a spiral staircase—with their hands in their pockets; but an Italian couldn't read a page of a Blue Book without gesticulation. It is as though the Latin hand were an independent organ of speech. This constant need of the hands to fortify conversations is perhaps one of the reasons why the Latin people so seldom have them in their pockets: that, and the circumstance that most Latin men carry purses. In England the purse is rare among men,

99

Encounters and Diversions

Among the various privileges of hands, the jingling of money in trousers pockets surely ranks high ? I am certain that no small part of the dejection which, on a recent visit to Austria and Germany, I noticed in the countenances of the men in those countries is due to the circumstance that they have no money to jingle. Paper money they have in profusion—paper money that used up my multiplication table very swiftly and left me gasping—but nothing to jingle. The jingling of money confers independence and authority on a man ; the jingling of too much money leads to arrogance—but the risk perhaps is worth running.

I don't know whether an illustrated book about hands in pictures by the great masters has ever been prepared, but it would be of interest. Some, it is well known, paid little attention to them ; Van Dyck, for instance, gives all his sitters the same hands, long and graceful and usually in the same posture— surely a very curious piece of carelessness on the part of one who must have been interested in character ? But that he knew a great deal about hands is proved by the studies that he made ; in Brussels there is a frame of them.

The Voice of the Hand

Rembrandt was as far opposed to this neglect, or disdain, as could be, the hands in all his portraits being hardly less important than the features, and being always accurately drawn. In the picture erroneously called " The Night Watch," the hand of the man in the middle seems to be thrust right out of the canvas. That picture is in Amsterdam. If you want an example nearer home of Rembrandt as a painter of hands, there is his " Parable of the Unmerciful Servant " at the Wallace Collection.

The early religious painters of Italy had a convention of hands and gave all the saints and the Madonna the same. Perhaps Botticelli's are as beautiful as any, but they lack any special quality beyond length and slenderness and the suggestion that no work was ever done by their possessors more exhausting than folding them in ecstasy, or holding babies and flowers. The sculptor, Mino da Fiesole, made the longest fingers of all. Leonardo was perhaps one of the first painters to consider hands worthy of thought ; but then Leonardo was first in so many ways. The hands of the Virgin in the picture called " The Virgin of the Rocks " in our National Gallery are lovely, but Leonardo's

IOI

masterpiece as a painter is the extended hand of Christ in " The Last Supper," at Milan, the moment being that in which He tells the disciples that one of them is to betray Him.

There are many beautiful hands in the National Gallery ; those of the Virgin in Piero della Francesca's " Nativity " at one extreme of unstudied simplicity, and at the other the hands of the tailor in Moroni's famous portrait. The hand of the man sitting at the table in Peter de Hooch's " Interior of a Dutch House " is admirably drawn, and if you look at it closely you will see that it once held the glass that has now been given to the woman by the window.

Palmists, I suppose, are born and not made, or I might try to qualify. I always envy the professors of this mystery as they settle down to their occult task. I don't know what is the attitude to it of the Fellows of the Royal Society, but my own experience of palmistry comprises some very extraordinary results. Total strangers have read in my hands secrets that I alone could have told them. And why not ? Surely if the Creator could make Darwin tulips and peacock butterflies, the chambered nautilus and the starry heavens, it may be conceded that

The Voice of the Hand

He could also, if He liked, amuse himself by writing our lives on our palms?

But if palmists are under suspicion, manicurists most certainly are not, and I consider them to be envied, too. Manicure is an excellent profession for a girl; it is not exhausting, it brings her intimately into association with a number of people, among whom a few must have something to say worth hearing, and she is devoting her time and thought to making those beautiful things, hands, more beautiful. A very worthy life! Perhaps her tragedy, however, is that she misses the people who don't go to manicurists.

Two Financiers ◇   ◇   ◇   ◇

"IT is in no spirit of boasting," he began, "no trafficking with what is known as swank, but solely in order to pave the way to the incident to be related, that I say that the other day I gave a beggar half a crown."

At this very impressive opening we all sat up prepared to listen closely. Half a crown is a great sum.

"It was an absurd experience," he said, "and I dare say there were better ways out of it than I took. Perhaps you will tell me."

We made noises intimating that most of our lives were spent in telling people about better ways than they have taken. At least, I did.

"It was like this," he said. "I had come up to Town for the day, my first place of call being at Islington. Now Islington is an unknown country to me. Beyond the fact that bailiffs have daughters there, I knew nothing.

Two Financiers

So I took a cab at Liverpool Street and gave the driver the address—an office. Well, the miracle of London traffic again occurred and we got there all right ; but while I was having the usual struggle with the window—this taxi having no inside door-handle and the driver being firmly nailed to his seat—a man hurried forward and opened it for me.

" At the same time he proffered a box of matches and forced me to look at him. Now, I don't set up for being one of the soft-hearted generous sort——"

Cries of " Oh ! "

" No, I don't. But this fellow really touched me. He was down and out. He was very shabby, very thin and haggard. Had been gassed, I should think, and was still periodically a victim. But the worst thing was his eyes. His eyes' settled it. They had a depth of pleading in them such as—well, such as in a well-organized world one man should never see in another's. It was awful.

" Of course I had to give him something, so I put my hand in my pocket, took out the only coin there and presented him with it—half a crown. I admit to being rather shocked

myself when I realized what the coin was ;
but I gave it to him."

Murmurs of approbation.

" But if I was shocked the man was stunned.
Expecting only a penny, he was overcome with
joy and retired swiftly to a neighbouring doorway to collect his feelings and debate upon
the best way to employ his fortune.

" Meanwhile I took out my pocket-book to
find something for the cab-fare, which was
two shillings ; and, behold, I had left it at
home. I hadn't any money at all. I had
given away my total capital. Now what would
you fellows have done ? That is the problem.
What would you have done ? "

" I," I said, " should have entered the premises
I had come to visit and have borrowed the fare."

" I tried to," he said, " but the place was
locked. No one there."

" I," said another man, " should have given
the cabman my card and promised to send
him not only the fare but a little more."

" I hadn't got a card," he said. " My cards
and my Treasury notes dwell normally in the
same pocket-book : the cards for a long while,
the notes only on the briefest visits."

" It's quite simple," said another man. " You should have pawned your watch."

" No, I couldn't do that. My watch is too sacred. It was given to me."

" Then," said I, " why not have got back into the cab and told him to drive to the nearest place where you were known and could borrow money ? Money you had to have sooner or later, anyway."

" I know. I suggested it, but the driver wouldn't do it. You know how independent they are. Either his home was near by, or one of those uncontrollable desires to eat an irregular meal, to which cabmen are so subject, came upon him. Anyway, he refused. Also, he had contrived at last to un-nail himself from the box and was beginning to look ugly ; and I hate that. I would do almost anything rather than have a row with a cabman in a crowded street. So what do you think I had to do ? "

" You don't mean to say," said some one in awe-struck tones, " that you asked the beggar to give you the half-crown back ? "

We all leant forward and held our breath.

" Yes," he said, " I did. It was the only course left. He was still in the doorway arranging the wonderful day that would begin when 'they opened,' and I went up to him. I never felt so ashamed in my life; and I believe it's the first money I've borrowed for thirty years."

Sounds of astonishment and incredulity.

" It's true. Somehow I've managed not to have to. I'm not boasting; I'm merely keeping to the point. Well, I faltered up to him, and I said, ' I'm most awfully sorry, but I've got to ask you to give me that half-crown back.'

" I shall never forget the expression on his face. Something like terror as well as pained surprise.

" I explained the situation, and the ghost of a smile crossed his lips. ' Of course,' he said, ' it's a pleasure to help anyone in distress. I know what no money means '; and he handed me the coin."

" Good man! " we said. " And then ? "

" Oh, well, then I found another cab whose driver was unaware of my financial status and I drove to my bank as fast as he could go."

" And the beggar ? " I asked.

" Didn't I say? Oh, he went with me, of course."

The Continental Dictionary ⌒   ⌒

AMERICANS.—Americans are people who prefer the Continent to their own country, but refuse to learn its languages. It is to Paris that, as a reward, dead Americans go who were good in life ; but one can also meet there Americans who must have arrived under false pretences.

ANSWERS.—Continental answers are very difficult to understand.

BILLS.—Long and bewildering documents made out in purple ink in which 4s look like 7s and 7s like 4s and 5s like nothing on earth, but which added together come to something simply appalling.

BILLIARDS on the Continent is less a form of religion than a game. Spectators at matches are allowed to talk. The balls are big and heavy and without any particular shape ; the cues are like jumping poles ; the tables are small, and there are no pockets. Often there are ninepins in the middle, and anyone who wishes to cut the cloth may do so. There is no such nonsense as a penalty for a miss.

BIRDS.—Most of the little singing birds on the Continent are seldom seen till they leave the kitchen. In Italy it needs several to make a dish for an adult.

BOOKS.—Continental books used to be much less proper than ours ; but we are catching up. They are not, however, so easy to read as ours. They usually need a dictionary, always need a paper-knife and are never bound in anything but paper. This means that the book-binders have a good time. Continental novels are always in their five hundredth thousand.

BREAKFAST.—There is no breakfast on the Continent, but Englishmen order two eggs.

BRIGANDS.—These are no longer the picturesque fully-armed ruffians who lurked in woods and lived in caves and held you up to ransom ; but they still exist in large numbers, wearing frock-coats or tail-coats and managing hotels.

CABMEN.—Since the introduction of the taxi-meter, these enemies of Society are less danger-ous than they were ; but the traveller who

The Continental Dictionary

cares for peace and quiet still gives them all
his small change too.

CHANNEL CROSSING.—Now that the three
railway systems that convey us to France
have combined and competition has vanished,
we must await the construction of the Channel
Tunnel with more fortitude than ever. Meanwhile, in wet weather only the very strongest
should dare the journey.

All the interest in the comfort of their passengers that is shown by the railway company
between London and the harbour, disappears
directly the harbour is reached. From that
moment the elements are allowed to take
charge.

The complaint against inventors, that they
spend their time and ingenuity on the wrong
things, is never found to be so just as on Channel crossings. The want of protection from
the weather ; the want of system in embarking
and disembarking the passengers ; the want of
system in embarking and disembarking their
personal luggage ; the want of any order in
the Custom-House rooms on either side, so that
they are now like the Rugby scrum ; the want
of cabin doors that will remain shut or open ;

III

the want of machinery that will take the boat direct into Boulogne harbour instead of pausing outside to turn, often in the worst sea ; in short, the want of consideration for anyone on board except the officers, is a continual scandal.

Take the matter of gangways alone. Surely there could be many ? But no, the harder it rains, the more, I have observed, do the officials cling to the tradition of the single gangway. Few sights are more depressing than the first glimpse of a rough sea in a gale, as one gets it from the train at Folkestone and Dover. But there is one sight that is even more miserable and provocative of that sinking feeling, and that is the solitary crowded gangway, slippery and set at an angle of forty-five degrees, by which all the thousand passengers • have slowly and uncomfortably to gain the ship.

I don't wish to be a spoil-sport, but I think the porters on both sides of the Channel, covered with bags and alpenstocks, for carrying which they are going to be far too heavily paid, get too much pleasure in using indiscriminately the steps from the top deck to the lower. Not only going down, but up. Couldn't an order be issued making these steps " one-way " ?

The Continental Dictionary

And what about the immense distance, without any protection from the weather, from the steamers to that inhospitable row of benches presided over by the amiable gentlemen who refuse to accept an Englishman's word? I am thinking in particular of Dover, but the height of discomfort seems to have been aimed at in all the ports. At the end of a bad crossing, to be again exposed to the elements after what we have the right to think of as dry land is reached, can be the final ordeal, and then to have our bags rummaged for a shillingsworth of *Eau de Cologne*!

Let there be a Channel Tunnel, and let it be soon!

CHICKEN.—The chicken—in all its manifestations, young, old, male, female and egg—is the Continent's best friend. In England it is still something of a state dish, and you will ask for it in vain at more inns than not; but on the Continent no *auberge* or *trattoria* is too small to produce either a *poulet* or a *pollo*, with an omelette to precede it.

"O hen," I should say, were I a poet in the mood for an ode—"O hen, we don't much admire your silly face; we are ashamed of your greed; we are pained when you run away and refuse to be friendly ; we hate the noise you make ; we hate even more the noise that your husband makes ; but we can't get on without you. You can always be relied upon to fill a gap, one way or another. We like you roasted, we like you grilled, we like you spatchcocked, we don't in the least agree that ' a chicken boiled is a chicken spoiled ' ; we think that without assistance from you a *risotto* wouldn't be worth having. Many a time and oft, after a long day's tramp or a mountain ascent, or even a motor run, you have saved our lives. You come to the rescue when beef is tough and mutton underdone, and even more so when there is no meat in the house. For you have the priceless merit of adjacency. Other food has to be bespoken, but there you are !

" And, O hen, your fruit ! What should we do without eggs ? It is an excitement to find them, it is a joy to eat them. We like them boiled (four minutes for mine), we like them fried, we like them poached ; best of all we like them with bacon. But bacon is better at home, O hen, than on the Continent. In France they call it *lard* (the shame !) and are

The Continental Dictionary

sparing with it; in Italy they call it *lardo* and are even more sparing of it. For eggs and bacon as they should be, England is the only place. In Holland they know about them but serve them too dry. "Yes, O hen, O chicken, for you in all your manifestations, we must seek the Continent!"

Thus, were I a poet, I should sing. But I am no poet, and so you must either be left unsung or the service must be performed by Mr. Yeats (who won the Nobel Prize for less), or Mr. Bridges (who invented the Great Silence), by Mr. A. E. Housman or Mr. Kipling, by Mr. Binyon or Mr. de la Mare, by Mr. Squire or Sir Henry Newbolt.

CHURCHES.—English travellers on the Continent are liable to severe shocks of surprise on finding that the churches are open all day and every day. It is even possible here and there to enter the chancel of a cathedral without having to pay a fee.

CIVILIZATION (FAILURE OF).—See Channel Crossing.

CLARET.—This beverage on the Continent is served stone cold, unless you particularly ask that it should be warmed.

Encounters and Diversions

COLLARS.—No scientific man or philosopher has ever yet been able to explain why the button-hole at the back of a Continental collar is horizontal, while that of an English collar is vertical. A man can become an F.R.S. and still have no theory as to this astonishing disparity.

COMIC PAPERS.—Continental comic papers have the same pictures every week, and, even if the words underneath them are changed, it is the same joke. Were there no underclothes there would be no comic papers.

CONCIERGE.—Whatever fluctuations may occur in the government of the countries of Europe —though Kings or Kaisers fall and anarchy reigns—the concierge will still be in control. Nothing can shake the power either of him or his wife. They sit at the door by day and move their bed to the door by night. They see all and hear all. They know who enters the house and who leaves it. They cannot be put off with falsehoods. If they don't like you they can make your life a burden ; and, if they don't dislike you they can do so too. Money can placate but never buy them.

CONSULS.—No one has ever seen one of these

The Continental Dictionary

elusive creatures. The most he has seen is an underling who is sorry the Consul isn't in and can't say when he will return.

CORRIDOR.—This is the part of a Continental train reserved for those passengers to whom, as they stand conversing or looking at the scenery, it comes always as a shock, very reluctantly realized, that other persons should want to pass.

COURIERS.—A courier is a man whose profession it is to look out slower trains and engage worse rooms than anybody else.

CROUPIERS.—Men in black coats and black moustaches who have never been to bed.

CUSTOMS-HOUSE.—A Customs-House is a place where otherwise scrupulously truthful men say they have nothing to declare. When the officer finds their cigars they say that their fool of a servant must have packed them against orders ; but as they cannot speak the language the officer does not understand, and if he did he would not believe it.

DISCOMFORT—See Channel Crossing.

ELEMENTS (EXPOSURE TO). — See Channel Crossing.

EXPENSES.—These are always rather more

Encounters and Diversions

than three times what you had calculated they
would be.

FOREIGNERS.—It is a great shock to many
English people on the Continent to find that they
are foreigners ; but it rarely causes them to revise
their opinion of those creatures on returning home.

GUIDES (DAY).—Day Guides are elderly men
with appealing eyes and baggy umbrellas who
know the year when Raphael was born.

GUIDES (NIGHT).—Night Guides should be
avoided.

ILLNESS.—It is very unwise to have an illness on the Continent. Nothing is so resented
there as sickness and especially the sickness of a
foreigner.

INTERPRETERS.—Interpreters are known as
such because the word " Interpreter " is on
their caps ; otherwise you might think of them
as almost anything but linguists. They are
useful as buffers between you and the rapacity
of porters and cabmen ; but in the end it costs
you more.

INVENTORS, THEIR MISDIRECTED INDUSTRY.
—See Channel Crossing.

LANDING-TICKET.—The piece of cardboard
that you lose while you are being sea-sick.

The Continental Dictionary

LIQUEURS.—It is possible on the Continent to be given over-measure of old brandy or other liqueurs and not be charged for it. Nothing of the kind has ever happened in England.

LUNCH.—This is the best meal of the day. It can begin as early as eleven and last till three.

MOSQUITOES.—Flying insects with a damnably poisonous bite which every one except hotel-managers has seen, heard and suffered from.

MOSQUITO-NETS. — Superfluous protections against mosquitoes which are " absolutely unnecessary, but you can, of course, have one if you insist."

MUSIC-HALLS.—In England and America the music-hall is popular, largely because the performance, having begun at the advertised hour, goes on without a break, or with one interval of very brief duration, till the end. In the Continental music-hall there is a considerable pause after every turn, and in the middle of the evening so long a pause that one wonders if the band or the scene-shifters have struck.

In Austria and Germany the music-hall audience on the ground floor and in the boxes

dine during the performance ; the others drink
beer.

In Italian music-halls few people listen and
there is no applause, but a performer now and
then learns from the decreased volume of cat-
calls and hisses that he has displeased the
audience less than most.

In Italian music-halls a popular song is sometimes sung as often as three times in one evening
by different singers, which indicates how lightly
the Italian showmen take their task. Such a
lapse in England or America would turn a
manager's shirt-front black.

OFFICERS.—Nothing is so astonishing about
the Continental officer that you see in the streets
and cafés as the friends he is with.

OLD MASTERS.—Although London has the
National Gallery and the Wallace Collection,
Londoners look at Old Masters only when
they are on the Continent.

OYSTERS.—English people, accustomed to
oysters that are dead and dry and very dear,
are surprised to find that Continental oysters
are often cheap and are always served fresh
and alive, in the deep shell, with their juice
still in them.

The Continental Dictionary

PASSPORTS.—Largely obsolete documents which, in spite of this widely advertised obsolescence, you must still line up in a queue on each side of the Channel to display to officials who don't look at them.

PAVEMENTS.—Pavements on the Continent are used not only for people to walk on but as dining-rooms.

PLATES.—When these articles are judged to be sufficiently cold, hot meat is served on them.

PLATFORMS.—There are no railway platforms on the Continent, with the result that every passenger must also be a mountaineer.

PORTERS (HOTEL).—Hotel porters come from Switzerland and never go back. They are big and blond and speak English, and are so wealthy as to be superior to tips. They are always on duty, always smart, and they can attend politely to ten people at once, draft a telegram, look out a train, change a five-pound note, ring up the occupant of a room and tell you also what hour a theatre begins, all at the same time. If they remained in Switzerland, Switzerland would be the leading country of the world.

Encounters and Diversions

PORTERS (RAILWAY).—Continental porters, besides being dressed in blue, differ from ours also in their disdain of barrows. English porters rejoice to keep us waiting while they " fetch a barrow," and as at all the great stations, by some careful arrangement by the general manager of the line, there is only one barrow to every ten porters, we are often kept waiting for a very long time. While an English porter is fetching a barrow the Continental porter has produced a strap and is binding your luggage together preparatory either to lifting it to his shoulder or crawling underneath and gradually rising more or less erect with it all over him, according to the weight. It is nothing for a Continental porter to carry in this way, by one strap, one innovation trunk, three portmanteaux, two kit-bags, a dressing-case, a tea-basket and a pair of skis.

POSTE-RESTANTE.—This is the department in Continental post-offices where travellers' letters are kept from the traveller by casual clerks smoking cigarettes. All Continental post-offices are run mainly in the interests of the tobacco trade, but in no department is smoking so steady. It is possible to believe the hotel

The Continental Dictionary

porter who says there is no letter for you, but one never has confidence in the thoroughness of the *Poste-restante* attendant.

POSTMEN.—An English postman never under any provocation advances beyond the front-door mat, but on the Continent a postman with a registered letter enters your bedroom and wakes you up and produces an ink-pot and pen in order to get your signature.

PROGRESS (WANT OF).—See Channel Crossing.

QUEUES.—No true European respects the queue, even though it has a French name. The last to arrive often sees to it that he is the first served.

RACE MEETINGS.—At Continental race meetings there is complete silence until the horses are near the winning-post or a jockey is thrown at a water-jump. Bookmakers do not exist, and you may leave your field-glasses on a chair confident that they will remain there. On the other hand, *pari-mutuel* prices are very small and you don't get your stake back.

SALTSPOONS.—There are no saltspoons on the Continent.

SECRETS.—The principal secret of travellers on the Continent, and particularly in Paris, is the name of " the best little restaurant you ever dreamed of—simple, I admit, but with the most wonderful wine and cooking." But when you reach it, it has either disappeared, changed hands, or " gone down."

SILENCE.—There is no silence so profound as that which envelops you when a Continental train stops in the small hours.

SLEEPING-CARS.—The sleeping-cars, known in France as *wagon-lits*, in Spain as *wagon-camas*, in Italy as *carrozze di letto* and in Germany as *schlaf wagen*, are possible only if you are rich enough to secure a whole compartment for yourself. You may then arrange your luggage, undress and dress with some degree of comfort. The trouble about them is that they have nearly always been engaged by other people ; and it is, of course, other people who are the traveller's cross. At every turn he is up against them. For if you are fortunate enough to get a berth it is made intolerable by the man who occupies the one below you. If you get a whole compartment you have to hear the other people washing. They are always washing when you want to wash, and there are no more towels. Also they are always

The Continental Dictionary

having their beds made when you want yours to be made. Conductors of *wagon-lits* always do more for other people than for you.

Only very strong people should travel by *wagon-lit*, because you have to push your luggage through the window.

Wagon-lits have more buttons and switches than anyone has ever discovered the meaning of. Just as dawn comes you find the one that turns on the light. *Wagon-lits* are divided into two berths, upper and lower. Hospitals are full of travellers who have tried to get into the upper.

Wagon-lits have no ventilation, but there is a little window at the top that admits the smuts.

SPRINGS.—The things which ought to be under your *wagon-lit* but have perished.

STATIONS.—Mysterious places where one wakes up in the *wagon-lit* and hears the brakes sigh.

STRING.—The tenuous substance with which Italian porters tie up trunks and bags that are already safely closed and locked.

STUPIDITY.—See Channel Crossing.

SUGAR.—Were it sweet, sugar on the Continent might be excellent.

Encounters and Diversions

THEATRES.—Theatres on the continent differ from ours in being very difficult to get into. Here the managers welcome patrons, but there they set them the task of getting past three men in top-hats in the lobby, whose duty and joy it is to take away your ticket and discuss it together. After a while, unless they dislike you very much, they give you another, which several other persons have to see before it passes into the hands of an elderly woman of forbidding aspect who consents to show you your place only on the receipt of a bribe. As, when you are really in the theatre the play is in a language that you can't understand and probably had much better not understand, it is better to sit over dinner.

TICKET COLLECTOR.—The man who never wants to see your ticket unless you are asleep.

TRAMS.—Unless the street is too narrow for tram lines, many Continental municipalities do not lay them. They then fit the tramcars with bells and tell the drivers never to stop clanging.

WAGON-RESTAURANTS.—There is no meal on a visit to the Continent so good as that in the first *wagon-restaurant*. Afterwards they deterio-

126

rate. They are staffed entirely by ex-jugglers. No tip has yet been produced large enough to persuade the chief official to let you change your seat. There is a point on the line between Calais and Boulogne where the curve is so sharp that you always get the next man's soup.

WAITERS.—Waiters are the principal inhabitants of the Continent. There are in the cities a few people not in evening dress by day, and in the country one is aware now and then of a peasant; but waiters are everywhere. They rise with the lark and retire with the owl, and in the interim never sit down.

WAITERS (WINE).—On the Continent the wine waiter does not have to be sent for, but is at your side as you sit down.

WINDOWS.—Things which " il est dangereux de se pencher au dehors " and " pericoloso sporgersi," Also from which, in Germany, there must be no outside-leaning.

WIVES.—Wives are useful on the Continent because they learnt French and Italian and German at school, and their husbands didn't.

The Critic ∽ ∽ ∽ ∽

IN the days when I used to write poetry I
had a literary friend who wrote short stories
intended for the magazines, and we dined at
the same chop-house not very far from Piccadilly
Circus. That was a long while ago, before
motor-cars, before cinemas, before tubes, when
few people had the telephone and none the
gramophone. And yet we did very well. When
we could afford it we jingled home in a hansom,
now and then exchanging a joke through the
roof with the cabman, which no one has ever done
with a taxi-driver. And though there was no
cinema there was Elizabeth Ann Bellwood singing
at the Tivoli, or Paul Cinquevalli juggling at the
Pavilion, and Wyndham was at the Criterion and
Irving at the Lyceum, and Regent Street stood.

The peculiarity of our chop-house was the
extreme deliberation of the waiters. There
were only two, and if it were possible for either

of them to be slower than the other, he was. It was only on the understanding that you, so to speak, accepted their tardiness that you were served at all ; but once having established yourself as a customer you remained. There is something hypnotic in leisurely processes : you were drugged ; but there were such positive advantages too, as the excellence of the food when it did arrive, the excellence of the beer, the sweet reasonableness of the charges, and the fun of watching strangers, unaware of the special guarded character of the place, getting angrier and angrier, and at last flinging out. In a word, if you were going to the theatre, it was the worst eating-place in London ; if you wanted to talk, it was the best.

I remember one evening awaiting Mark, as I will call him, with no little excitement, because I had just finished a poem and I thought sufficiently well of it to wish for his praise.

" I wanted to see you," I said. " I've written some verses which I rather think you'll like. About dreams," and I took the manuscript out of my pocket.

" Talking of dreams," he said. " I've just finished a story about one. Very odd you should have brought it to my mind like that. I should like to tell you about it. In fact, I happen to have the first draft with me, and we might see if we can't improve it while we eat."

I placed rather carefully beside my plate the sheet of paper on which my poem was written. " It's astonishing," I said, " what trouble even a short lyric can give one ! No one reading this "—and I tapped it—" would believe that I spent three hours on one of the four stanzas."

" I don't know," he said. " I always feel that rhymes help you. Now, in writing a story you get no help. The art of the short story is one of the most difficult to master. But I flatter myself——" Here he disappeared for a few moments behind a tankard—" I flatter myself I'm getting near it. This story "—he deposited his exhibit on the table too—" this story is about a man who dreams futures. He lives in a village and has got a terrific reputation for his gift. You go to him and impress your personality on him in some way——"

" If you've got one," I suggested.

" Yes ; don't interrupt, please. Of course, if you've got one. And then he dreams about you. Well, my story is about one of these dreams. A girl goes to him and he dreams a future for her, and she can't frustrate it. It's very uncanny. In fact "—he glanced at himself in a mirror with some satisfaction—" I can't think how I thought of it. ' We are greater than we know '—how does the line go ? Anyway, it's about this girl that I think you might possibly be able to help . . ."

I won't bother you with any more of the story. Suffice it to say that Mark was still picking my brains when we suddenly realized how late it was and hurried off just in time to see Harry Pleon, who came on that week at the Pavilion at 10.35.

The next time we met, at the same place, I had a triumph to display : my poem had been accepted and I had the evening paper containing it in my pocket.

" This is the dream-lyric I wanted to show you a week or so ago," I said.

He read it :—

ALTRUISM.

My nights among the dead are past ;
   When sleep at last is here
Into my dreams come thronging fast
   The friends of yesteryear.

Encounters and Diversions

They share the wild absurdities
    That mark the dreamer's track,
Caprice controls their entrances ;
    But ah ! I've brought them back.

Nor I nor they display surprise,
    Familiar is their shape ;
I wonder if they realize
    And relish their escape ?

If so, then let us sleep the more,
    To help them, over there—
Our friends not lost but gone before—
    To constant change of air.

" Not bad," he said as he handed the paper
back. " I like it better than when you showed
it me first."

Friendship's Offering ~ ~ ~

IT was in those careless far-off days when
we were all beginning, and were pledged to do
what we could for each other, that we used to
meet at the Gate House on Hampstead Heath
(where knives and forks used by Dick Turpin
were kept in a glass case), and, either in one of
the arbours, or upstairs, according to the
weather, compared notes and planned campaigns.

It is of one of the more shameless of those
campaigns that I would tell.

Among us was one whom I will call Tommy
Ridler (now an illustrious publicist). To him
Fortune had been less kind than to some of us,
and he had got not even one toe on the ladder ;
nothing that he wrote was accepted.

As I have said, we were all pledged to help
each other, and on the evening that I am recalling,
Dick Struthers (also now well known by another
name), who had just come back from a holiday

133

on the Norfolk Broads, was talking about the birds there.

" Now, take the corncrake," he said. " That's a rum 'un if you like. It makes a row all day and half the night, and no one's ever seen one yet."

" Nonsense," said I. " They have them in museums."

" Maybe," he said. " But museums don't count."

" Still they had to be stuffed," I said. I was argumentative in those days.

" Taxidermists don't count either," said Dick. " Speaking generally, no one has ever seen a corncrake. Jolly interesting, isn't it ? "

Even I agreed.

" Look here, Tommy," he went on, " why don't you mug up the corncrake in some book and write about it. That's the kind of thing editors like : facts about a mystery, even if the mystery's only a blooming bird. Give your inventive powers a rest for a few minutes and try information for a change."

And Tommy did so. He found out all about the corncrake, otherwise known as landrail, one of the *Rallidœ*, the *Rallus crex* of Linnæus, and all the rest of it. He dug out of the classics the legend that it was the corncrake or landrail that was the *Ortygometra* which led the quail on its voyages. He described its self-protective colouring (see Mimicry in Nature) ; its ventriloquial powers, so that you never know in which direction it is ; its haunts ; its eggs, usually eleven in number, laid in a nest in the long grass ; and the whole bag of tricks. And what is more, he got the article accepted.

There it was, in our favourite hunting-ground for guineas, *The Globe and Traveller* : " The mysterious Corncrake—From a Correspondent." Not a " Turnover "—Tommy's style was not flexible enough for that—but an inside column.

" Splendid ! " said Dick when he heard the news. " Now we must get busy and rub this in. Tommy's future as the popular ornithologist must be made."

" Is ornithology a necessity ? " Tommy pathetically inquired. " You've no notion how I loathe birds."

" Of course," said Dick, " you must continue as you have begun. You must be identified in the public mind with our feathered friends. Specialisation, you know. That's the art of success."

Encounters and Diversions

And he outlined the campaign.

During the week the Editor of *The Globe and Traveller* received the following missives :—

THE LAURELS,
TUNBRIDGE WELLS.

DEAR SIR,—My husband, who is a well-known medical man and amateur ornithologist, is deeply interested in the article on the Corncrake which you printed last week. He would much like to be put in touch with the author, if that is permissible, and he hopes that you will be able to give us more of his admirable work.

I am,

Yours faithfully,

SELINA PARRISH.

107 TRUMPINGTON STREET,
CAMBRIDGE.

DEAR SIR,—You have, if you will allow me to say so, discovered a real treasure in the contributor who writes on the Corncrake. I have rarely read anything more fascinating than his account of that strangely elusive bird. It would be a boon to me personally if you would invite him to give you a series of articles on other of our stranger birds, such as the wood-

136

Friendship's Offering

cock, the snipe and, say, the hawk family, of which too little is known.

> I am,
>> Yours faithfully,
>>> MARCUS GROW.

THE NOOK,
> HAMPSTEAD HEATH

DEAR SIR,—You can't think what a pleasure you gave to my family and myself by that article on the Corncrake. If only there was less about politics and divorce and police and more about nature, how much sweeter would the papers be! Please get this fascinating Correspondent to write again.

> Yours sincerely,
>> AGATHA THORN.

8 LINCOLN'S INN FIELDS, W.C.

DEAR SIR,—Kindly forward the enclosed letter to your Correspondent on the Corncrake. It is not written to attempt to lure him from your literary staff, but to congratulate him on a first-class piece of work and wish him health and strength to continue.

> Yours faithfully,
>> AMBROSE HEARTY.

137

Encounters and Diversions

ST. FRANCIS'S COLLEGE,
EASTBOURNE.

DEAR SIR,—Your article on the Corncrake is just what we want in school, and I hope you will have more. My boys are all keen on birds.

Believe me,

Yours faithfully,

HENRY SWIFT.

UNITED SERVICE CLUB, S.W.

DEAR SIR,—I shall be grateful if you would kindly favour me with the name and address of your correspondent who writes on the Corncrake. I am preparing a work on migratory birds and should much value the assistance of his knowledge and literary skill.

I am,

Yours faithfully,

(Lieut.-Colonel) HUGO DUNDAS.

SEA-SCENT,
BOURNEMOUTH.

DEAR SIR,—Speaking with my uncle, the Vicar of Dewfield, the other day, he said that, in a long experience as a reader of ornithological books and articles, he could not remember a more informing or interesting paper than that in a recent number on the Corncrake. The Vicar is now in his eightieth year and very feeble in everything but intellect, and it would be a kind act on your part to arrange for further articles by the same writer as a solace to his declining days.

I am,

Yours faithfully.

LUCY SPEARING.

Need I add that all those letters and many more were written by Tommy's four friends either the same evening or during the next few days, and arrangements made with friends or relations for the postmarks to be correct? Not bad, were they? One even was written by the disgraceful hand of Tommy himself. Can you guess which? The last. Oh, Tommy!

But the sad thing is, they didn't take the Editor in.

A Romance of To-morrow ᘓ ᘓ

MANY years ago, when I first came to London, I saw a good deal of a man named Purvis. He was about thirty—older than any of us, round, bearded, jocular, imperturbable, and apparently he lived like the lilies. He kept no hours, was always on hand if anyone was being festive, and the fair fame of literature, English or French, seemed to be in his keeping. His talk was always of books and authors, and there was a rumour that he was a writer himself. It was this rumour—unsupported, I must admit, by any evidence—that gave him his place in our respect ; for the young who are themselves thinking of plying the precarious pen look with dilated eyes upon those who have already achieved print.

One day—it must have been in 1892—he confided to me that he had the most wonderful idea for a novel and was about to draw up the

scenario. Other ideas had come to him before
but they had been disappointing ; this was the
real thing. This was what, he now knew, he
had been saving himself for ; this was terrific.
If henceforward I saw less of him than usual I
should know the reason : he would be wrest-
ling with the plot, endeavouring to control the
mighty primeval forces that were being let loose.
For this was to be a human drama of the fiercest
elemental passions : a tragedy of the country-
side. The provisional title was *Herodias Valling*.
He would say no more about it then, he added,
but from time to time he might ; although it
was a mistake to talk about what one was
projecting.

A little later I received an invitation to attend
at Purvis's rooms one evening to join in the
ceremony of laying the foundation-page of a
new novel. For, as he argued when we were all
assembled, why should not the beginnings of
works of art be celebrated just as much as
buildings ? With more propriety, surely, for a
work of art may live for ever, whereas buildings
fall into ruin. He would ask us all to drink to
the prosperity of the sheet of paper on the
table. A number of bottles of champagne, not

a very good brand—and champagne, anyway,
no matter of what vintage, is a hateful beverage
between meals—were then released ; we filled
our glasses; we lifted them; our host turned
over the sheet of paper, revealing the title,
Herodias Valling, a tragic novel, by Rutland
Purvis ; and we drank the masterpiece's health.

Purvis then lit a pipe and told us the plot.
Like all jovial facetious men, he had a leaning
towards the melancholy and macabre, and this
story was one of unrelieved gloom. From early
childhood Herodias's surroundings were sinister.
The house was half ruined ; creditors were
always threatening ; her step-father never spoke ;
her mother only whimpered ; nettles and deadly
nightshade overran the garden ; owls occupied
the attics.

But Herodias managed to grow in this dismal
environment into a girl of surpassing loveliness.
From this point onwards the story bore (to my
mind) too close a resemblance to a much-dis-
cussed novel of the day, by a pactised hand,
called *Tess of the d'Urbevilles*, on which we had
all heard Purvis express himself again and again,
usually with unstinted appreciation.

As he continued the outline he became more

and more moved ; his voice broke, his eyes
filled with tears ; and at the end, when Herodias
committed suicide in a gravel-pit, he was a wreck.
It was a very uncomfortable and impressive
moment, and we all avoided each other's gaze
and found ourselves thinking of Purvis with
renewed and deepened respect. There must, we
realized, be something very fine underneath that
mask of levity. All the same, I couldn't forget
Tess.

Although we sat on for some time, for there
were still bottles to empty, Purvis never re-
covered his natural gaiety, and when he said
Good-night and received our best wishes once
more, he pressed our hands with almost painful
gratitude and understanding. Henceforth, we
felt, we were to be in this great work too, and
were his collaborators in the tragedy which was
to dissolve England in grief.

The next time I saw Purvis he was his normal
self. It was on my tongue to make a reference
to the great work, but I checked the impulse ; I
felt that so grave a subject should be introduced
by the author or not at all. Purvis talked of
everything else, and we went to Lord's.

The next time I saw him he said that the

distractions of London were fatal to the development of great tragic themes and he was going to the country, to be solitary, where he might give his imagination rein and work out his drama in uninterrupted peace. Such a book needed seclusion. Perhaps, when he had broken the back of it, I would come down and see him ?

I said I would, and a few months later I went down. He was in Sussex, and he met me at the station as merry and debonair as ever, with the usual big pipe. I must be prepared, he said on the way, for the people I was to meet, for he was living *en famille* with a farmer and his daughters, two very nice girls. Miss Esther and Miss Kate.

" And the novel ? " I asked.

" I'll tell you about that," he said, "later."

Anything less like the hermitage that he had proposed to flee to, anything less like a lodge in the wilderness, I never saw than Gleesome's Farm. The farmer was a sly humourist who made Purvis a constant butt ; the daughters were jolly tomboys. Our dinner was one long laugh. Purvis had a sitting-room of his own, but it would be more sociable, he said, to be with the others ; so after dinner we played " Snap " and

A Romance of To-morrow

" Families " and other childish games till it was
time for bed. " Time for bed," when Purvis
was in London, was a phrase without meaning,
but now he yawned and lit my candle.

After breakfast the next day I said I would
go for a walk so that Purvis might get on with
his work, but he said he would come too. On
the walk he told me again the plot of *Herodias
Valling*, and again became emotional over it ;
but when I asked if he had not some chapters
that I might see, he said that so far he had done
very little. The moment had not arrived.
" One must wait," he said, " in matters of this
kind, till the clock strikes."

All that was thirty or more years ago, and
I completely lost sight of him. Either he did
not return to London or our lives ceased to cross.
But last week I met him again. He was older,
grey, less jaunty ; but I knew him at once.

" I've been looking for that novel all this
time," I said. " But if it has come out under its
original title I've missed it."

" Fancy your remembering ! " he said. " No,
it hasn't been published yet. I'm still at work
on it. One mustn't hurry a thing like that."

The Bottle's Progress ∽ ∽ ∽

(With pictorial assistance from Mr. Frank Reynolds)

ALL adventurous amateurs of London, and especially the young, have a period in their lives when there is no excitement equal to the discovery of a new and remarkable Soho restaurant. It may be French, it may be Italian, and it is sometimes Spanish ; but whatever their alleged nationality all are alike in being extraordinarily good and extraordinarily cheap, and "For heaven's sake, old man, keep it to yourself, because if you tell every one, the place will be ruined ! "

Another peculiarity which these little restaurants share, and which is not perhaps an advantage, is the absence of a licence, so that all wine has to be fetched from a neighbouring shop or public-house.

It was in one of these restaurants (the name of which I would not give away under any con-

146

The Bottle's Progress

sideration) that I was sitting when two young men entered and sat down at a neighbouring table. Mine was by the window commanding the street; theirs was farther in.

I had no need to strain my ears to learn that the host was of the centre, and the guest a beginner in Bohemia.

Having ordered the food they came to the question of the wine.

" You like St. Emilion ? " the host asked.

Yes, he liked St. Emilion.

" You always get good St. Emilion in Soho," said the host. " We'll have a bottle. Warms you."

He chose a brand and paid for it—for that, as you know, is the rule in these places—and a young waiter in old evening clothes was sent off to get it.

" Be careful with it," the host called out.

" Yessir," said the boy.

" A mistake to shake good claret," the host explained to his friend.

" Is it ? Yes, of course," said the friend, and they settled down to confidential talk, which I neither heard nor wanted to hear.

It was then that the cinema operator should

147

Encounters and Diversions

have begun to turn his handle, for this, as I could see through the window, is what occurred.

The young waiter entered the public-house at the corner and came out with the bottle, holding it like this :—

The Bottle's Progress

At this moment he met a friend, also a waiter, from another marvellous little restaurant on

the same errand, and the friend took the bottle and examined it, holding it with equal negligence.

Encounters and Diversions

As the two youths parted, the second of them gave the first a friendly blow and ran away, and our waiter pursued, brandishing the bottle on high like a club.

The chase ended at the public-house door, when our waiter again turned homewards.

He was nearly home when still another waiter,

The Bottle's Progress

bent on the same errand and obviously in a hurry,
arrived and, glancing at the bottle and seeing
that it was the same brand that he too had

been sent for, asked to be allowed **to have** it.
I could not, of course, hear, but they came both
of gesticulating parents, and the conversation

was as plain as though spoken to me. " I'm in
a hurry and you're not," his hands distinctly said.

Our waiter, however, very properly refused
to relinquish the bottle, whereupon the other

seized it, and a terrific battle for its possession
set in, which, with a terrific wrench, our waiter

won. He then slipped into the restaurant and behind the *caisse*, where the bottle was un-corked and otherwise dealt with. And this is how it emerged—

The host sipped the wine critically. "Ex-cellent!" he said. "Perfect condition."

Joe ∽ ∽ ∽ ∽ ∽

From Stephen Dunk, farmer and churchwarden, to Mr. Septimus Rose, scholar and recluse, the new tenant of The Grange, Pulham

DEAR SIR,—We should be grateful if you would give something in aid of the Pulham bellringers.

I am,

Yours obediently,

STEPHEN DUNK

Mr. Septimus Rose to Mr. Stephen Dunk

Mr. Septimus Rose is not a lover of church bells, which, of course, should have disappeared when clocks and watches became cheap ; but, since the custom of ringing them persists, he encloses a ten-shilling note.

Mr. Stephen Dunk to Mr. Septimus Rose

DEAR SIR,—I beg to thank you for your subscription to the bellringers. I note what you say about clocks, but I would respectfully

154

point out that whereas clocks and watches are often fast or slow, the Pulham bells keep time. I can promise your ears some rare treats on practice nights as well as on Sundays.

I am,

Yours obediently,

STEPHEN DUNK

Mr. Septimus Rose to Mr. Stephen Dunk

Mr. Septimus Rose would like the leader of the bellringers to know that last evening's practice, so far from being a rare treat, was notable for a very obnoxious discord causing him to regret having made any contribution to the funds.

Mr. Stephen Dunk to Mr. Septimus Rose

DEAR SIR,—With reference to your letter about the ringing, all I can say is that I am the leader and that I think it must have been Joe Grover ; but you must kindly remember that Joe is new to the bells and unless he practises he'll never learn. We all do our best, but in the nature of things Wednesday evenings can't be as perfect as Sundays. A nicer lad than Joe doesn't breathe, as you, Sir, would be the first to agree if you met him. If you will kindly have patience you will soon have no cause to complain again. I have the honour to be

Yours obediently,
STEPHEN DUNK

Mr. Septimus Rose to Mr. Stephen Dunk

Mr. Septimus Rose is perfectly willing to take Joe Grover's merits as a lad on hearsay, but his ringing is atrocious. Mr. Rose suggests that for a few weeks Joe practises in some other village.

Mr. Stephen Dunk to Mr. Septimus Rose

DEAR SIR,—With reference to your further letter about poor Joe, I am afraid you do not quite appreciate the position. It is one thing to practise with your own ringers and quite another to practise with strangers. In point of fact, Joe would be useless to our peal if he practised anywhere but at Pulham, and, if I may be allowed to say so, Sir, we must all learn. Joe will be a fine ringer one of these days, he has the strength and he has the will.

I am,
Yours obediently,
STEPHEN DUNK

156

Joe

Mr. Septimus Rose to Mr. Stephen Dunk

To Mr. Dunk's last letter, Mr. Septimus Rose
would say that when he settled in Pulham it
was for peace and quiet, and he gave his subscription to the bellringers because he considered
himself one of the community. He did not
then know, as he now does, that bellringing is
a disease here. The " rare treats " that his ears
were promised have been nothing but assaults.
In his opinion bellringing should be kept for
Sunday, although he is convinced that Sunday also is better without it. If Mr. Dunk will
arrange to confine all ringing to Sundays Mr.
Rose will increase his subscription to a pound.

Mr. Stephen Dunk to Mr. Septimus Rose

DEAR SIR,—With reference to your letter
about practice and ringing on Sundays only, I
am sorry to say it is impossible. The week-
day practice has been going on for years, maybe
for centuries, and such an ancient and honourable custom could not be tampered with on
any account, and certainly not for ten shillings.
Moreover, the inhabitants, many of which have
lived here a long time, have come to expect
it. I am sorry, but there it is.

Encounters and Diversions

And another thing, Sir, how could we promise to ring only on Sundays when there are such things as weddings, which are nothing without a peal, and funerals, where tolling is expected? In fact much of our practising is done for weddings, which is the only time when we get something extra for ourselves.

No, Sir, I am sorry, but we can't change the practice day. I think you'll find a difference next Wednesday evening. Joe is coming along nicely.

I have the honour to be,

Yours obediently,

STEPHEN DUNK

Mr. Joseph Grover to Mr. Septimus Rose

DERE SIR if you will give to me the ten bob instead of to the others I will send in my resignashun.

Yours truely,

JOSEPH GROVER

Mr. Stephen Dunk to Mr. Septimus Rose

DEAR SIR,—With reference to your letter about the choir practice, I hasten to inform you that you are not likely to be troubled again, as Joe has retired. We shall miss the lad, for

Joe

he was willing and regular, but he says he was never sure that ringing was his true calling, and so he is joining the choir, having a fair baritone voice. We are trying young Horace Peters in Joe's place, with hopes for the best, but I am afraid he will take a lot of training. From your point of view I expect it is a pity Joe left.

I have the honour to be,

Yours obediently,

STEPHEN DUNK

59,654 ✤ ✤ ✤ ✤ ✤

I WONDER how many people could guess without any assistance what the number at the head of this article signifies. I believe it would be safe even for me to offer a large monetary prize to anyone providing a correct answer.

I have put it to all kinds of persons and they have hazarded ingenious theories.

" I know," said one man instantly : " it's your ticket in the Calcutta Sweep."

" No," I said.

" It's something to do with Reparations," said another.

" No," I said.

" It's too high for a telephone number," said a third man.

" Yes," I said.

" And too low for your income."

I disregarded this remark.

" It might be the number of the hairs of your head," he mused.

I disregarded this too.

" It's the number of marks or crowns or roubles you got for a pound when you were in Germany or Austria or Russia," suggested another.

" No," I said.

" Well, I'm glad it's not," he replied, " because I'm so tired of that kind of talk."

It was then that I began to throw lights. " It refers to something to eat," I said.

No one was inspired.

" You couldn't guess," I said, " unless you had been abroad."

No response.

" The number," I said, " occurs on a picture-post card."

Still no one had an idea.

"The picture," I went on, "represents an elderly man with whiskers engaged in a culinary occupation."

Their eyes remained dull.

" You," I said, pointing to the man who had been boasting that he knew Paris backwards, " doesn't that tell you ? "

" No," he said sulkily.

" Then I will throw more light," I said. " The number was written in by the successor of the elderly man with whiskers, and the card was then presented to me as a souvenir. Does that illumine the darkness? No? Then let me add that the scene is the oldest restaurant in Paris, and that the culinary operation is the slicing of a duck preparatory to crushing the carcass. And now you know. The duck served to me on the occasion of my last visit to the Tour d'Argent was the 59,654th."

" Of course ! " they each exclaimed. " How stupid of me ! "

And then we fell to the discussion of this famous resort of the epicure and the gourmet, not to mention the gourmand.

You seek the Silver Tower for the flesh of the duck—the best ducks that the fair land of France can produce, served with quintessential sauce extracted from their own bones. Some one is always carving a breast, some one is always turning the handle of a press, some one is always catching the juice, some one is always eating ; everybody is always talking.

" It's an amusing place," I said, " and you ought to go there once on every visit to Paris ; but it isn't so good as it used to be."

" Nothing in Paris is," said one of the company.

59,654

" For one thing," I said, " they are now putting too much lemon in the sauce. For another, they are too noisy. You see, it's a very small room, and it isn't as if your duck —I mean my duck—No. 59,654—was the only one. Far from it. While I am waiting for mine No. 59,653 is having the finishing touches put to it, and they are beginning on No. 59,655 and No. 59,656. That means that four fat men are beating up sauce in four metal dishes over four spirit-lamps all together. The din, even apart from the conversation of the guests, many of whom are strong silent Americans, is deafening. Now, I like to eat quietly. To go to the Tour d'Argent because it was founded in 1582 and has no band, and then to find it like a boiler-works, is very disconcerting. No quality of duck can compensate for that."

" The Tour d'Argent," said the man who knew Paris, " has another point of interest which renders it unique among Paris restaurants —it is always closed on Mondays."

" Why ? " asked some one.

" To let the staff consult their aurists," he said.

Another Derby ∽ ∽ ∽ ∽

*From Mr. Jonah Punt to Sir Benton Stakes, owner of
Apogee, the favourite*
                                    May 25, 19—.

DEAR SIR,—Permit a stranger, actuated by
none but the best motives, to bring some facts
to your notice.

The Derby is to be run in a fortnight and
you are the owner of the favourite. From all
that I know of the horse, its pedigree, its form,
its owner, its trainer and its jockey, Apogee
ought to win. The opinion of the best judges
is also to this effect.

I have no doubt that you have backed the
horse yourself ; but even if you haven't you
stand to make a large sum from the prize,
and also from the possession, later on, of so
valuable a sire.

Another Derby

My object in writing to you is to let you know that unless you acquire my co-operation you cannot win. No owner can win any race if I care to intervene, because my influence is irresistible. I don't go so far as to claim that my intervention can force a horse to come in first, but I do emphatically say this, that it can prevent a horse from doing so ; and it is because I want you to win the Derby with Apogee that I am writing to you now.

Briefly, you must pay me not to bet on him, because if I back him he will lose. Every horse that I back loses. But, as hope springs eternal in the human breast, I go on backing them. I am, however, prepared not to do so if you will make it worth my while. If you will send me five hundred pounds I will put a small amount on every runner but yours and keep the balance.

I adjure you to give this letter serious attention. It may look fantastic, but is not. Every horse that I back loses.

I am,

Yours faithfully,

JONAH PUNT.

165

Encounters and Diversions

II

From " The Seer's " Notes in " The Daily Wire "

The news of Apogee gets better every day and I am told that his gallop yesterday morning resembled nothing so much as streaked lightning. It will be difficult to get 2 to 1 on the day of the race.

III

From Captain Allright's Notes in " The Morning Telegram "

If ever a Derby could be said to be a cert it is the one to be run next week. Nothing but some disastrous accident can prevent Apogee from winning. The son of Apollo and Gee-whizz is probably the fastest colt that ever entered for this race.

IV

From Latest Prices
THE DERBY
Apogee evens

Another Derby

V

From Colonel Knut's Notes in " The Turf Oracle "

It would not surprise me if Apogee were to start odds on, but even then I advise my readers to bet fearlessly. We have this year such a chance to skin the pencillers as has never arisen in the chief of the Classics.

VI

From Dick Turpin's Notes in " The Evening Wire "

I am told that every man, woman and child connected with Apogee's stable is on the horse, and that Sir Benton Stakes, who invested huge amounts on the colt last autumn, when the price was long, is still backing him even at the present pinched rates. Confidence in horses has ruled high before and has been found to be misplaced ; but I am prepared to put my only shirt on Apogee.

VII

Mr. Jonah Punt to Sir Benton Stakes

May 30, 19—.

DEAR SIR,—I am astonished to have received no reply to my letter of the 25th. It was a

167

perfectly serious document, written in good
faith, out of the wish for you to add the Blue
Ribbon of the Turf to your name. I am not
a blackmailer or even a beggar; I am simply
your friend, who would like to have some
recompense for his thoughtfulness. Five hundred pounds is nothing to a man who is about
to win the Derby; to me it would be useful.
And one thing is certain : if you don't pay
it you can't win. There is no question whatever : horses that I back lose. I have your
Derby in my hands. A speedy reply is necessary
if you wish to succeed.

I am,

Yours faithfully,

JONAH PUNT

VIII

*From the Notes by " The Thunderer's " Special Racing
Correspondent*

For the great race of to-day there seems
to be no necessity to look farther than Apogee.
This fine speedy colt was never in better fettle,
and he will start with the perfect confidence
of owner; trainer and jockey. That J. Primus

has the mount is an additional reason for assurance. Having previously subjected, with perhaps tiresome iteration, the various candidates to the minutest examination, I need not again repeat my reasons for ruling all of them out. One no doubt will come in second, and one third. The winning horse will be Apogee.

IX

Mr. Jonah Punt to Sir Benton Stakes, on Derby Day Morning

(Reply Paid Telegram)

This is your last chance to stop me. If you don't reply before noon I back Apogee.

PUNT

X

Paddock Wire, Morning of Race

Apogee is in perfect condition and cannot lose.

XI

Mr. Jonah Punt to Duggie Lurem

Apogee five shillings win.—PUNT

Encounters and Diversions

XII

Every paper heading on the afternoon of the race :—

DERBY SENSATION.
OUTSIDER WINS.
APOGEE NOT PLACED.

XIII

Telegram from Mr. Jonah Punt to Sir Benton Stakes

I told you so. My bad luck is invincible.

He and She ～　～　～　～

*H*E. I have just heard that she is coming by the noon train. This is great news. I must go and make everything ready for her.

*   *   *   *

Her name, the letter says, is Chloe. I don't like that. I must think of another ; something attractive but short ; something one can call out loud and sharply.

*   *   *   *

" Tess," wouldn't be bad. I think I'll call her Tess.

*   *   *   *

Yes, Tess.

*   *   *   *

She (*in the train*). I wonder where I'm going. This is very uncomfortable. It shakes horribly.

*   *   *   *

Encounters and Diversions

I hate being alone, too.

* * * *

I wish I'd been kinder to mother.

* * * *

I wonder if they've got any shooting. Mother will be disappointed if they haven't.

* * * *

Poor mother.

* * * *

He (*on the platform*). She's a beauty. I never saw such silky black ears, such a splendid coat.

* * * *

But she doesn't seem very friendly. Not a single wag has she given me yet.

* * * *

She. I don't care much about him ; in fact I don't like him at all. I hate having my head patted.

* * * *

I don't care for his trousers.

* * * *

Or his boots.

* * * *

He and She

His hand smells of tobacco.

    *   *   *   *

He. This is very disappointing. I was hoping for a real companion ; looking forward to it. And she's terrified of me. Won't come near. Hides under the furniture if I approach.

    *   *   *   *

Well, perhaps she's nervous from the journey —the strangeness of it all.

    *   *   *   *

She. I don't care for this place a bit. There's no other dog and no one to talk to. I hate fences all round.

    *   *   *   *

I don't like him a bit. He's a feeble creature ; no character. I hate people who are always coaxing me to come to them. It's degrading.

    *   *   *   *

I shall concentrate on the cook.

    *   *   *   *

LATER.

The cook's a great disappointment. A vegetarian household, I'm afraid ; at any rate, no meat comes my way. Soaked biscuit and

173

Encounters and Diversions

cabbage—what's the use of that? Well, if I don't eat it they'll have to give me something better. Nothing like hunger-striking to make them nervous, and one must begin right. Poor mother always said that.

* * * *

Dear mother.

* * * *

I wish I'd been kinder to her.

* * * *

He. She's adamant. I can't get her to come within three yards, and then she's all suspicion. And the worst of it is she's so dainty. You can usually get at a dog through its greed; but not this one. I suppose if I tried raw beef it would be all right; but I don't care for such bribery as that, and the breeder's letter said on no account give meat.

* * * *

She. I was so hungry to-day I had to eat the biscuit. I'm furious about being so weak-minded, but one must live. The funny thing is it didn't taste so bad. Still, it was a mistake, and now perhaps I'll never persuade them and so never get any meat at all.

* * * *

He and She

He. I'm having rotten luck. To-day after lunch she let me approach my hand almost within an inch, and then a log fell and she rushed in alarm to the other end of the room. She thought I did it. Any unusual sudden frightening sound she blames me for.

*   *   *   *

I've never been so disappointed.

*   *   *   *

I always thought that spaniels were so affectionate.

*   *   *   *

She. He still follows me about with his hand held out to me, making silly murmurs. It's sickening. How I dislike him!

*   *   *   *

He. This morning a terrible thing happened. Tess ran into the field and caught a young chicken belonging to the farmer. If dogs pursue chickens it is, of course, fatal, so I had to be very severe. After ten minutes spent in pursuit I caught her and lashed her with a switch until she screamed.

*   *   *   *

It was dreadful, but I had no option.

*   *   *   *

Encounters and Diversions

Spare the rod and spoil the dog.

* * * *

But that, of course, settles it. She'll never come near me again. I may as well send her away and get another for all the comfort she'll ever be to me.

* * * *

She. I'm so sore. My sides are that tender I can hardly bear to lie down, and I'm too miserable to stand up. The fact is I worried a chicken. I was bored to death, and there the little idiot was—you know what fools chickens are—and so I grabbed it. It was only for fun ; but the way those people carried on ! And then HE came out with a lady's riding-whip and after no end of a chase caught me. I knew I was for it sooner or later, but I decided I'd lead him a dance.

* * * *

How he puffed and panted !

* * * *

And then he began to lay it on. My tail, but it hurt ! I yelled and yelled, but he went on and on until I really began to admire him in spite of myself. I didn't know he was so

176

He and She

masterful. I expected him to stop directly I screamed. But he went on and on until his arm must have ached.

*   *   *   *

And then he flung me away.

*   *   *   *

He. The most wonderful thing in the world has happened. She's sitting in my lap, licking my hand!

" Norbury Jack "   ᴂ   ᴂ   ᴂ

I T was shortly after " Norbury Jack," the Airedale, had received, on May 17th, 1923, the bronze medal of the National Canine Defence League for giving warning of fire, that a number of his fellow dogs met to decide upon what was the best form of honour that they too could offer him. Ordinarily, said the Chairman, a champion Mastiff, it was agreed by human beings that a dog's virtue should be its own reward, but on this occasion a little imagination had entered into the case. The action of the National Canine Defence League did credit to their articulate two-legged friends. (Hear, hear.)

The chairman then reminded the meeting of " Norbury Jack's " claim to distinction.

It seemed that on the night of April 18th attention was drawn to the blazing of the outhouses by the clamour which he raised. But for that timely assistance the whole place would have been destroyed.

The Collie said that, though no doubt it was gratifying to see human beings alive to the intelligence of dogs, this seemed to him a rather trivial performance for so much attention. What dog was there in that room, who, in the presence of a rapidly encroaching fire, would not utter sounds of alarm ? To make a row under such conditions was practically automatic. (Oh, Oh !) He was not trying to underrate " Norbury Jack's " action ; he was merely suggesting that it was not a matter for any special excitement on their part. The medal was putting a premium on a purely instinctive action. Had " Norbury Jack " refrained from making a row, that would have been, if not precisely praiseworthy, at any rate remarkable. He personally was opposed to carrying the matter any further. (Groans.)

The Irish Setter here sprang to his feet to say that he totally disagreed with the last speaker, who, like most Scottish dogs, was cold and parochially and pedantically logical. (Hear, hear !) If merit were always measured in that frigid and mechanical way, the world would not be worth living in. He moved that " Norbury Jack " be invited to as rich a banquet as could be arranged. (Loud cheers.)

The Greyhound said he should like to second that.

The Skye Terrier said that there was a great deal in what his friend and compatriot the Collie had put before them. Fire was such a terrifying element that few dogs could forbear from running screaming from it, and a sense of self-protection would probably cause them to run in the direction of their masters. None the less it was an admirable thing for the master to recognize the value of such a warning. A medal was all very well as a permanent token, but for real appreciation he, the speaker, was in favour of the banquet as well.

The Clumber Spaniel said that what they had to remember was that it was just as easy for a dog frightened by a fire to lose his head completely and run away from his owner, as towards him, and that in the present case " Norbury Jack " had run instantly towards his owner. That was the peculiar excellence of this case. Let there by all means be a banquet.

The Collie, asking leave to speak again,

repeated that he had no animus against " Norbury Jack," but he was against facile sentiment. He was, however, wholly in favour of the banquet.

The St. Bernard, who had come all the way from Switzerland to attend the meeting, said that he was delighted to hear of an Airedale winning a medal for assisting mankind. The circumstance that such altrusim was a daily occurrence with himself did not detract from the merit of the deed. He hoped that the banquet would be arranged, and arranged quickly, as he should like to stay for it.

The Bedlington said that he should throw himself bodily into the banquet scheme.

The Newfoundland said that he agreed with the St. Bernard. He was glad to welcome the Airedale to the ranks of the life-savers.

The Aberdeen said that he had come to the meeting expressly to suggest a banquet.

The Yorkshire Terrier said that though his capacity was small he hoped to do justice to " Norbury Jack's " heroism.

The Pomeranian said that he hoped there would be a banquet, but would take it kindly if there were no plum-pudding.

The Lurcher said that there were conceivable

cases where a dog of spirit would be doing his only true duty if he allowed his master's house to burn down. He himself had a master so brutal and exacting that no calamity could be too severe for him.

The Chairman here interrupted to say that, interesting as was the last speaker's experience, it hardly bore upon the situation.

The Lurcher apologized for being so passionately personal and expressed his entire approval of the project of giving " Norbury Jack " a banquet.

The Sealyham, who claimed to be the most popular dog of the day, said that he would gladly extend his patronage to the banquet.

The Spaniel said that the notion of a banquet appealed to him.

The Pekinese (who was accompanied by a Chinese interpreter) said that in his country a dog's chief duty was to its parents and ancestors, but here, he had noticed, parents and children were quickly parted, usually for ever. An English dog normally never saw its father at all, and its mother only for a few weeks. If a dog had neither father nor mother to care for, it was right and proper to be solicitous about owners and, if necessary, to give notice of fire. He was in favour of a banquet, and hoped there would be snipes' livers, as those were expressly mentioned by the best Chinese authority on the dietary of Pekinese spaniels. (Sensation.)

The French Poodle said that he had often done things quite as noteworthy and probably even more heroic than " Norbury Jack," but no one had recorded them. Heroism, he had observed, had got to happen at the right moment —that is to say when some one was looking— or it was in danger of being called duty. None the less he should register a vote for the banquet.

Other dogs having expressed their views in similar terms, the Chairman said that it seemed to be the wish of the majority that there should be a banquet and it was not necessary to take a show of tails. It only remained to appoint a small committee to carry out the arrangements. This the meeting was proceeding to do when I left.

Windfalls ～ ～ ～ ～

RECESSIONAL

THE world now and then—praises be!—goes backward.

Hugh, who is four years old, lately left his perfectly appointed London home for a few days at a seaside town where some of the most recent improvements are lacking.

His mother went down for the week-end, to see how the place was suiting him, and Hugh and his nurse were at the station.

"We've got the most exciting thing in our house you ever saw," he said.

"What is it?" his mother asked.

"No," he said, "it's a secret. You'll see it this afternoon, just before tea." He jumped for joy.

Just before tea the great moment came and with it the triumph, the novelty.

The gas was lighted!

Windfalls

" And where do you go for your holidays ? "
I asked him.

" We don't go anywhere," he said. " I can't
afford it. And I don't care about it very much
either. Lodgings are not comfortable."

He resumed his attack on my thinning locks.

"Every one should have some kind of change,"
I said.

" That's right," he replied. " And we do.
We've got a little plan of our own that's like a
holiday and isn't one ; it gives us a change and
doesn't cost anything."

I asked for the solution.

" It's very simple," he said. " You'll laugh
at it. But it's this : we just exchange bedrooms.
There's my wife and myself and my son and my
daughter. Three rooms. Well, we exchange.
We move the furniture and the pictures, and
there you are. You wake up in the morning
and look out of a different window. The door's
in a new place. It's a change."

" And are your family satisfied too ? " I asked.
"Your son and daughter? Don't they want the
seaside or the country ? "

" No," he said ; " they're quite happy. But

185

sometimes they ask if they may re-paper their walls, and I let them. That makes a change too."

LIFE

Once upon a time, on a gusty day, a man was counting his money in his car, and one of the notes blew away all unknown to its owner.

It lodged unseen in the wet grass at the side of the road, until by and by two wayfarers came along. One of them was a millionaire returning from the neighbouring golf links ; the other was a wretched old woman faint from hunger. It was the millionaire who, preceding her by a few yards, found the note.

BREAD ON THE WATERS

Uncle Roland, home from the East, was on his first visit to his married sister since the boys were mere mites, and he made himself very popular. When it was discovered that his birthday was on November 2 the boys clubbed their pocket-money to give him a present worth having, as a mark of their very great esteem. They gave him five shillings'-worth of fireworks.

Windfalls

THE BAD INFLUENCE

I was calling, the other day, on a friend—one of the gentlest of men, gracious, considerate, unselfish—and suddenly his telephone bell rang. I asked, as I always do, if I should leave him alone while he answered it, but he said No, and I remained.

I wish I hadn't, for I received the shock of my life when he suddenly exploded into a fury and attacked some other unfortunate telephoner who was talking across him.

" Get off the line ! " he screamed, his face purpling with rage.

When he had put back the receiver he apologized.

" I'm awfully sorry," he said. " It's a most distressing thing, but the telephone has that effect on me. I can't restrain myself. I am normally placid and easy-going, tolerant of other people's irritating ways. But on the telephone I can't keep my temper. I chafe at delay, I fume at wrong numbers, I lose all my courtesy to women, and you heard me just now abusing that quite innocent offender. It's very serious ; it's shortening my life, souring my

13   187

nature. I am perfectly convinced that the
telephone is a mischievous institution, and in
the interest of sweetness and light it ought to be
abolished. How does it affect a courteous even-
tempered man like you ? "

" Just the same," I said.

THE PHYSIOGNOMIST

London, when she lost the hansom and the
four-wheeler, lost also the waterman ; for such
was the odd name by which the cab-rank attendant used to be known. His official position
was that of refresher of horses, but he gave
more attention to the duty of looking out for
fares, catching their eyes, holding the door open
for them with one hand and extending the other
for twopence.

We could do with the waterman now, for
taxi-drivers have a way of sinking either into
newspapers or slumber, and disregarding signals
of distress. But except here and there he has
gone. One, however, was on duty the other day
in Piccadilly, when a friend of mine—a man of
distinguished appearance and of some personal
pride—was passing along the Green Park side,
bent upon the economy of a bus to Kensington.

Windfalls

As he proceeded he was aware, not far ahead of him, of a smiling roguish fellow holding open a taxi-door, with every indication that it was for him that the civility was intended.

" Here you are, Sir," said the waterman.

" But I didn't hail you," said my friend.

" No," said the waterman, " but you've got a taxi-face."

And my friend stepped in.

The Reason

I was asking my attendant, the Italian, if he intended to go to his home city, Milan, for his holidays.

" No," he said ; " when my father and mother were alive I liked to go home. Now only brothers and sisters, and I don't. They think that every one in England is rich ; that you have only to stoop down to pick up gold. If I give them only a little money, they treat me as though I was a criminal. If I give them much, they expect more."

The Mind-Changer

My friend the lift-man wore a look of gloom. Usually so bright and talkative, he was now silent and depressed.

Encounters and Diversions

" Anything wrong ? " I asked.

" Everything," he said.   " I daren't go home."

" Oh, rubbish ! " I replied.   " Of course you can.   Why not ? "

" The missis," he said.

I admit that the reason might be a formidable one, but not in his case.   From all that he had led me to imagine, his home life was serene ; and I had seen the lunches she prepared for him. Thoughtful lunches.

" Tell me," I said.

He opened an evening paper and pointed to the four o'clock.   " Do you see what price the winner was ? " he asked.

I saw : 33 to 1.   " Great odds," I said.

" Yes," he replied.   " And the missis gave me half-a-crown to back it with."

" And you forgot ? " I suggested.

" No, I didn't," he said.   " I wish I had.   It was worse than that.   I changed her mind for her, and put it on something else—an also-ran.   And there she is, waiting, so excited, with over four quid to come—and I changed her mind for her.   Blimey, I'm not half for it ! "

Windfalls

A West African letter, the writer of which was smarting under an affront, real or imaginary, suffered in a Lagos bank :—

DEAR SIR,—Of necessity, I am compelled to complain to you Sir, the hautiness embossed on me some hours ago.

It came to pass that I appeared before the Cashier on the Counter this morning purposely to draw some amount and I, being hasty, invoked his attention which resulted in an insult from him with the most abusive word " silly " repeatedly ; which struck me to the utmost and blew me to an ague. And this insulter at once reported to the accountant, asked him to close my account simply to punish me prejudicially after having stained me respectability with unfair words.

I cannot pose as one possessing the authority to speak the faults of the staff but as a regular customer enjoying mutuality, and I believe if such a process does not receive a full stop which it deserves, it will be a means to suffocation to the progressive regularity of the customers and the advancement of the company.

The English language is far too limited to

adequately express how achy I feel when such an abuse was focussed on me.

I do not write to teach your worthiness what to do, but respectfully conjure a precaution to suppress such a practice.

Awaiting your justificaly reply,

I remain,

Sir,

Your obedient Servant.

———

I see no reason why the writer of that letter should abuse the English language for its inadequacy.

The Two Wives

Once upon a time there were two girls who married on the same day, and several years afterwards they met again.

" Is your husband kind ? " asked one.

" He's the kindest thing you ever heard of," said the other. " There's nothing he won't do for me. He is always buying me presents ; he thinks of my comfort continually ; he is unfailingly fond."

" Then you are happy ? " asked the other.

192

Windfalls

" Tell me about yours," she said.

" My husband isn't like that," said the other ;
" he is all extremes. He lost his money, and we
are not rich, like you, but very poor. And he
can be so violent. Sometimes he treats me
cruelly ; sometimes he doesn't speak for days ;
often he is drunk. I never know what to expect.
But then, when he is not beside himself, no one
can be so loving. His love is wonderful."

" I envy you," said the rich woman.

THE SECRETS

I was sitting at the bedside of a philosopher
aged and fragile.

" The secret of dying," he said, " is to grow
fonder and fonder of sleep."

" And of living ? " I asked.

" The secret of living," he said, " is to be
always ready for death, but far from eager for
it."